ARCHAEOLOGY FOR THE PEOPLE

Joukowsky Institute Publications

ARCHAEOLOGY FOR THE PEOPLE

PERSPECTIVES FROM THE JOUKOWSKY INSTITUTE

edited by

John F. Cherry and Felipe Rojas

Oxbow Books
Oxford and Philadelphia

Joukowsky Institute Publication 7

General series editor: Prof. John F. Cherry
Joukowsky Institute for Archaeology and the Ancient World
Brown University, Box 1837/60 George Street, Providence, RI 02912, USA

Published in the United Kingdom in 2015 by
OXBOW BOOKS
10 Hythe Bridge Street, Oxford OX1 2EW

and in the United States by
OXBOW BOOKS
1950 Lawrence Road, Havertown, PA 19083

Published by Oxbow Books on behalf of the Joukowsky Institute

© Brown University, Oxbow Books and the individual contributors 2015

Paperback Edition: ISBN 978-1-78570-107-8
Digital Edition: ISBN 978-1-78570-108-5

A CIP record for this book is available from the British Library

Library of Congress Control Number: 2015952702

Printed in the United Kingdom by Hobbs the Printers Ltd, Totton, Hampshire

For a complete list of Oxbow titles, please contact:

UNITED KINGDOM
Oxbow Books
Telephone (01865) 241249
Fax (01865) 794449
Email: oxbow@oxbowbooks.com
www.oxbowbooks.com

UNITED STATES OF AMERICA
Oxbow Books
Telephone (800) 791-9354
Fax (610) 853-9146
Email: queries@casemateacademic.com
www.casemateacademic.com/oxbow

Oxbow Books is part of the Casemate Group

Cover images: Part of a Soviet propaganda poster used in one of the advertisements for the *Archaeology for the People* competition.

Contents

Preface

Archaeology for the People was written by people who enjoy archaeology for people who enjoy archaeology. The book's main purpose is to showcase essays on archaeological topics written for a non-specialized audience. Although most of the contributing authors are practicing archaeologists, our intended audience is not primarily our own colleagues or students. In fact, the bulk of this book can be read with interest and pleasure, we hope, by anyone who cares about the material traces of the human past.

The essays that make up Chapters 2 through 8 deal with important questions that are being tackled by archaeologists today; their content, scope, and style are inevitably and thankfully diverse. They provide a taste of the variety and versatility of contemporary archaeological thought and practice. Some touch upon major moments in the history of our species: *Did agriculture precede organized religion, or was it the other way round? When did people first set foot in the Americas?* Others focus on specific cultural and temporal horizons (such as the late Maya world) and reflect on issues of contemporary interest (*How and why do cities cease to be viable?*). Yet others treat local problems involving the physical traces of the past in present-day urban environments and probe the relevance of an archaeology of the more recent past: *What are the material reflexes of apartheid on the fabric of Cape Town? What exactly is lost when historical urban garden plots in Istanbul succumb to financial and political pressures?* Two essays concern the willful damage done to archaeological sites by looting: *How can something good be salvaged from the violent destruction of a Native American site in the Ohio Valley? What can we learn from the troubled life story of a famous Greek vase?* If any or all of these questions intrigue you, this book is for you.

Chapter 9 involves minimal prose; instead, it uses photographs to capture some of the richness and challenges of everyday life on a remote archaeological site in Northern Sudan. This chapter too is meant for archaeologists and non-archaeologists alike. Chapters 1, 10 and 11, however, are a different matter. They are primarily aimed at professional archaeologists and at those who write about archaeology, although we hope that others too may find them of interest. These chapters all confronted a simple central question: how can archaeologists make the achievements and challenges of their discipline accessible to a non-specialized audience? Chapter 1 explains the editors' motivations for organizing an international writing competition that resulted in the essays presented in this volume. Chapter 10 discusses the experience of teaching what was, we believe, the first Massive Open Online Course (MOOC) about archaeology; in this chapter, the authors analyze the demographics and interests of those who enrolled in their MOOC and offer reflections about just who the people in *Archaeology for the People* may be. Chapter 11 gathers answers to a questionnaire that the editors distributed among a group of rare and exceptional persons – prominent archaeologists who have managed to write forcefully and effectively for people other than their peers.

We are convinced that archaeology deserves a vast and diverse audience and that it is our duty as archaeologists to reach all such people, wherever and whoever they may be. *Archaeology for the People* is our modest attempt at sharing some of the pleasure we derive from reading and writing about our intriguing, and important, field.

List of Figures

Notes on Contributors

Susan E. Alcock is Special Counsel for International Outreach and Engagement in the Office of the President of the University of Michigan, and was from 2006 until 2015 the Director of the Joukowsky Institute for Archaeology and the Ancient World at Brown University. She is a classical archaeologist, with interests in the material culture of the eastern Mediterranean and western Asia, particularly in Hellenistic and Roman times. Much of her research to date has revolved around themes of landscape, imperialism, sacred space, and memory. Her most recent fieldwork was at and around the site of Petra in the Hashemite Kingdom of Jordan.

Elif Batuman is a Turkish-American author, academic, and journalist who has written for the *London Review of Books*, the *Paris Review*, *The New Yorker*, *n+1*, and *The New York Times*. Her first book, *The Possessed: Adventures with Russian Books and the People Who Read Them*, was a finalist for the National Book Critics Circle Award.

Laurel Bestock is Vartan Gregorian Assistant Professor of Archaeology and the Ancient World and Egyptology and Assyriology at Brown University. Her research focuses on the material culture of the Nile Valley, with particular interests in kingship, monumentality, the development of sacred space over time, and cultural interactions. She conducts fieldwork at Abydos, in Egypt, and at Uronarti, in the Sudan.

John F. Cherry is Joukowsky Family Professor of Archaeology and Professor of Classics, Brown University. His teaching, research interests, and publications reflect a background in Classics, Anthropology, and Archaeology, as well as educational training on both sides of the Atlantic, and archaeological fieldwork experience in Great Britain, the United States, Yugoslav Macedonia, Italy, Armenia, and (especially) Greece and (currently) Montserrat in the Caribbean. He has published 140 papers and chapters, and co-authored or co-edited 12 books. He has been co-editor of the *Journal of Mediterranean Archaeology* for 25 years and is the General Series Editor for *Joukowsky Institute Publications*.

Chip Colwell is Curator of Anthropology at the Denver Museum of Nature and Science. He received his Ph.D. from Indiana University, and has held fellowships with the Center for Desert Archaeology, American Academy of Arts and Sciences, National Endowment for the Humanities, and US Fulbright Program. He has published nearly 50 articles and chapters, and nine books. His work has been highlighted in such venues as *Archaeology* magazine, *Indian Country Today*, the *New York Times*, *Slate*, and the *Huffington Post*, and has garnered numerous awards, including the National Council on Public History Book Award and the Gordon R. Willey Prize of the American Anthropological Association.

Kara Cooney is Assistant Professor of Egyptian Art and Architecture at the University of California, Los Angeles. She worked on two Discovery Channel documentary series: *Out of Egypt* and *Egypt's Lost Queen*. Her most recent book is *The Woman Who Would Be King: Hapshepsut's Rise to Power in Ancient Egypt* (2014).

J. Andrew Dufton is a doctoral candidate at the Joukowsky Institute for Archaeology and the Ancient World, Brown University, whose dissertation looks at the changes to North African cities under the Roman Empire, in particular how elite-sponsored spatial restructuring was received by non-elite populations. His research interests include urbanism and urban process, Iron Age and Roman North Africa, and a methodological focus on the uses of digital and web technologies for the dissemination of archaeological data and texts.

Müge Durusu-Tanrıöver is a doctoral candidate in the Joukowsky Institute for Archaeology and the Ancient World, Brown University. Her research interests mainly lie in the Bronze Ages of the Near East, with particular emphases on state formation, borderlands, memory, and place and place-making. Her dissertation explores how the Hittite Empire functioned within the long-term trajectories and landscapes in the margins of the empire. Durusu-Tanrıöver has conducted archaeological fieldwork in several regions of Turkey, most recently in central Anatolia with the Yalburt Yaylası Archaeological Landscape Research Project.

Keith Eppich joined his first archaeological project at the age of eight at Bedico Creek in the state of Louisiana, where he was raised. He has excavated Tchefuncte shell mounds, Pleistocene bone-beds, Antebellum plantations, Californian missions, Chumash camps, and ancient Maya cities. He holds degrees from Louisiana State University, San Diego State University, and

Southern Methodist University (Ph.D. dissertation 2011, *Lineage and State at El Perú-Waka': Ceramic and Architectural Perspectives on the Classic Maya Social Dynamic*). He is currently an Associate Professor at Collin College in Plano, Texas.

Brian Fagan is Professor Emeritus of Anthropology at the University of California, Santa Barbara. He is the author or editor almost 50 books, including a number of widely used college textbooks, and has extensive experience with the development of public television programs on archaeology, as an archaeological consultant, and as a public lecturer. Fagan was awarded the 1996 Society of Professional Archaeologists' Distinguished Service Award for his "untiring efforts to bring archaeology in front of the public." He also received a Presidential Citation Award from the Society for American Archaeology in 1996 for his work in textbook, general writing, and media activities.

Alfredo González-Ruibal is an archaeologist with the Institute of Heritage Sciences at the Spanish National Research Council, whose work now focuses on the archaeology of the contemporary past; he is co-ordinator of an archaeological project about the civil war and early dictatorship in Spain. His books include *La experiencia del otro* (2012), *Reclaiming Archaeology* (2013), *An Archaeology of Resistance: Materiality and Time in an African Borderland* (2014), and (with Gabriel Moshenska) *Ethics and the Archaeology of Violence* (2014).

Yannis Hamilakis has been Professor of Archaeology at Southampton University since 2000. Recent field projects in Greece have involved archaeological ethnography and excavation at Kalaureia (Poros) and Koutroulou Magoula. His 11 books as editor or author include *The Nation and its Ruins* (2007) and *Archaeology and the Senses* (2013).

A. Gwynn Henderson is Staff Archaeologist and Education Coordinator for the Kentucky Archaeological Survey and Adjunct Assistant Professor in the Department of Anthropology at the University of Kentucky. Her interests lie in researching Late Prehistoric and Contact Period farming cultures of the middle Ohio River Valley; working with archaeologists and educators to make information about Kentucky archaeology accessible to a wide audience; and writing for children and the general public.

Cornelius Holtorf has been, since 2008, Professor of Archaeology at Linnaeus University in Kalmar, Sweden. His books include *From Stonehenge* *to Las Vegas: Archaeology as Popular Culture* (2005) and *Archaeology is a Brand! The Meaning of Archaeology in Contemporary Popular Culture* (2007).

Marilyn Johnson, a former editor at *Esquire* and *Outside* magazines and a former staff writer for *Life*, is the author of three books: *The Dead Beat* (2009), *This Book Is Overdue!* (2011), and *Lives in Ruins: Archaeologists and the Seductive Lure of Human Rubble* (2014), which reached Amazon's list of Best 100 Books (Print).

Leonardo López Luján is among the leading researchers working on prehispanic Central Mexican societies and the history of archaeology in Mexico, with more than two dozen single-authored or edited books to his credit. He is director of the Templo Mayor Project in Mexico's National Institute of Anthropology and History.

Marta Ostovich is a Ph.D. candidate in the Department of Archaeology at Boston University, with a dissertation advocating a sustainable approach to the management of cultural landscapes. Her research interests include international heritage management, cultural tourism, and the archaeology of the Western Mediterranean

Colin Renfrew (Lord Renfrew of Kaimsthorn) was, until his retirement, the Disney Professor of Archaeology at the University of Cambridge and Director of the McDonald Institute for Archaeological Research. His many books include *The Emergence of Civilisation* (1972), *Before Civilisation* (1973), *Archaeology and Language* (1987), and (with Paul Bahn) *Archaeology: Theories, Methods and Practice* (1991).

Felipe Rojas is Assistant Professor of Archaeology at Brown University. He conducts archaeological fieldwork in western Turkey at the port city of Notion (in Ionia) and the mountain sanctuary of Labraunda (in Caria). He is currently writing a book about how the people of Greek and Roman Anatolia reinterpreted and manipulated the material remains of the Bronze and Iron Ages. His interests include the comparative history of antiquarian traditions and the archaeology and history of writing systems.

Nick Shepherd is Associate Professor of African Studies and Archaeology at the University of Cape Town, where he convenes the Project on Heritage and Public Culture in Africa. His books include the volume *Desire Lines: Space, Memory and Identity in the Post-apartheid city* (2007); *New South African Keywords* (2008); *After Ethics: Ancestral Voices and Post-disciplinary Worlds in*

Archaeology (2014), and *The Mirror in the Ground: Archaeology, Photography and the Making of a Disciplinary Archive* (2015).

Aleksandar Shopov received his B.A. and M.A. degrees in history at St. Cyril and Methodius University in Skopje and Sabancı University in Istanbul, and is currently a Ph.D. candidate at Harvard University. His dissertation contextualizes changes in the genre of farming books from the Early Modern Eastern Mediterranean, by connecting them to agricultural transformations within and around major urban centers in the region. His research draws from manuscripts and archival documents, written in Ottoman-Turkish and Arabic, preserved in Istanbul, Cairo, Paris, Sofia, Skopje, and elsewhere.

Vernon Silver is a Rome-based senior writer for Bloomberg News and author of *The Lost Chalice: The Epic Hunt for a Priceless Masterpiece* (William Morrow, 2009). He holds a doctorate in archaeology and a master's degree in anthropological archaeology from the University of Oxford. A native New Yorker, Silver graduated from Brown University in 1991 with degrees in political science and American civilization.

Chantel E. White received her Ph.D. in Archaeology from Boston University in 2013 and joined the Department of Anthropology at the University of Notre Dame as a Postdoctoral Fellow. Her paleoethnobotanical research (the study of ancient plants) has focused on understanding Neolithic and Early Bronze Age farming practices in Southwest Asia. She is also currently conducting archaeological fieldwork in Classical and Early Byzantine Greece.

Contributor Addresses and E-mails

Susan E. Alcock
Office of the President
University of Michigan
2064 Fleming Administration Building
503 Thompson Street
Ann Arbor, MI 48109
salcock@umich.edu

Elif Batuman
http://www.newyorker.com/
 contributors/elif-batuman

Laurel Bestock
Joukowsky Institute for Archaeology
 and the Ancient World
Brown University, Box 1837
60 George St
Providence, RI 02912
laurel_bestock@brown.edu

John F. Cherry
Joukowsky Institute for Archaeology
 and the Ancient World
Brown University, Box 1837
60 George St
Providence, RI 02912
john_cherry@brown.edu

Chip Colwell
Denver Museum of Nature and
 Science
Department of Anthropology
2001 Colorado Blvd.
Denver, CO 80205
chip.colwell@dmns.org

Kara Cooney
cooney@g.ucla.edu

J. Andrew Dufton
Joukowsky Institute for Archaeology
 and the Ancient World
Brown University, Box 1837
60 George St
Providence, RI 02912
andrew_dufton@brown.edu

Müge Durusu-Tanrıöver
Joukowsky Institute for Archaeology
 and the Ancient World
Brown University, Box 1837
60 George St
Providence, RI 02912
muge_durusu@brown.edu

Keith Eppich
Department of Social and Behavioral
 Science, Rm 247
Collin College
2800 E. Spring Creek Parkway
Plano, TX 75074
keithevaneppich@gmail.com

Brian Fagan
brianfagan1@cox.net

Alfredo González-Ruibal
alfredo.gonzalez-ruibal@incipit.csic.es

Yannis Hamilakis
Y.Hamilakis@soton.ac.uk

A. Gwynn Henderson
Kentucky Archaeological Survey
1020A Export Street
Lexington, KY 40506-9854
Aghend2@uky.edu

Cornelius Holtorf
cornelius.holtorf@lnu.se

Marilyn Johnson
marilynajohnson@gmail.com

Leonardo López Luján
leonardo@nauhmitl.com

Marta Ostovich
Department of Archaeology
Boston University
675 Commonwealth Ave.
Boston, MA 02215
martaostovich@gmail.com

Colin Renfrew
acr10@cam.ac.uk

Felipe Rojas
Joukowsky Institute for Archaeology
   and the Ancient World
Brown University, Box 1837
60 George St
Providence, RI 02912
Felipe_Rojas@brown.edu

Nick Shepherd
School of African and Gender Studies
University of Cape Town
Rondebosch
South Africa
nick.shepherd@uct.ac.za

Vernon Silver
vernon.silver@stx.oxon.org

Aleksandar Shopov
Center for Middle Eastern Studies
Harvard University
38 Kirkland Street
Cambridge, MA 02138
aleksandarsopov@gmail.com

Chantel E. White
Department of Anthropology
University of Notre Dame
611 Flanner Hall
Notre Dame, IN 46556
cwhite16@nd.edu

Introduction:
What Is Archaeology for the People?

John F. Cherry and Felipe Rojas

Initial version of the *Archaeology for the People* competition poster.

We can trace back the varied contributions in this volume to two origin-points: one quite generic, the other very specific. The generic aspect can be located in the mission statement of the Joukowsky Institute for Archaeology and the Ancient World, formulated at the time of the Institute's establishment in 2006. It reads:

> The Joukowsky Institute promotes the investigation, understanding, and enjoyment of the archaeology and art of the ancient Mediterranean, Egypt, and Western Asia, through active fieldwork projects, graduate and undergraduate programs, and public outreach activities.

The key words here are "enjoyment" and "public outreach," and we have tried, over the past decade, to fulfill this mandate in a variety of ways.

Some of the classes offered to Brown University undergraduates, for example, have had deliberately "sexy," come-on titles, such as *Troy Rocks!*; *Stealing History*; *Fake!*; *Pirates of the Caribbean*; and so on. Such offerings are intended both as "gateway" classes to stimulate an interest in taking further archaeology courses, but also as an enjoyable, one-time exposure to archaeology for those whose priorities as students lie mainly elsewhere. We have also regularly sponsored teaching to students in Providence-area public schools with a program entitled "Think Like an Archaeologist," which has in turn spawned comparable programs on Montserrat in the Caribbean (Ryzewski and Cherry 2012: 322–324) and in the Rochester, New York area (Archaeological Institute of America 2014). The Institute's most ambitious attempt to reach out to an extremely wide audience is undoubtedly the MOOC (Massive Open Online Course) "Archaeology's Dirty Little Secrets" which has now been taught twice to tens of thousands of enrollees, as discussed by Alcock *et al.* (forthcoming) and in Ch. 11 of this book.

The more specific prompt arose from the musings of some of us within the Joukowsky Institute about why there appears to be so little compelling and high-quality writing aimed at a broader community of readers interested in archaeology, but for the most part not professionally involved in it. One of us (FR), rather casually, sent out an email to members of the Institute to ask them what book or shorter piece of writing they felt was particularly effective in reaching this broader community. The pool of respondents was small and hardly representative; but their answers were revealing. Perhaps predictably, some of the responses fingered relatively recent best-sellers, such as *Breaking the Maya Code* (Coe 1992), *Guns, Germs, and Steel* (Diamond 1997), *1491* (Mann 2005), *Imperium* (Harris 2006), or *The First Human* (Gibbons 2006). Other titles included books aimed at a much more restricted readership, though certainly written in prose of great evocative power, sometimes combining poetic nostalgia with scholarly precision – for example, *Luminous Debris: Reflecting on Vestige in Provence and Languedoc* (Sobin 1999). More peculiar was the fact that about a quarter of respondents chose Marguerite Yourcenar's historical biography, *Memoirs of Hadrian*, published (originally in French) as long ago as 1951, and which is not, in fact, about archaeology.

These results, from an admittedly skewed and small sample, all archaeologists, led to some head-scratching. Why does it appear that there are so few good books out there that have been written in such a manner as to make them accessible to a non-specialized audience? Articles fared even worse. Our little survey threw up a few familiar titles that most of us have probably read and would acknowledge as well written, oft-cited, and influential – but influential only within the field of professional archaeology, and not at all outside it. There are of course archaeological articles of another kind, explicitly aimed at a broad audience: those that appear regularly in magazines such as *National Geographic, Archaeology, Biblical Archaeology, Archaeology Odyssey, American Archaeology, Popular Archaeology, Current Archaeology, Current World Archaeology*, or (for children ages 9–14) *Dig into History*, as well as more occasionally in established museum-sponsored publications such as *Smithsonian* and *Natural History*. These and other such magazines publish a huge amount of material on very frequent (monthly or bi-monthly) schedules, and in some cases their circulation is substantial (nearly a quarter million for *Archaeology* and over two million for *Smithsonian*, in both cases with even larger readerships). To generalize about them is probably unfair. Nonetheless, the archaeologically-themed pieces appearing in such venues tend to share certain recurrent features: (a) relative brevity; (b) a heavy emphasis on illustration, with pictures sometimes occupying almost as much space as text; and (c) a tendency to converge on certain tropes and themes. These especially include new, dramatic, or otherwise arresting finds; unsolved "mysteries" of archaeology (or, conversely, mysteries that archaeology may, allegedly, finally have helped solve); and a rather narrow range of perennially popular topics (such as the "riddle" of Stonehenge, or diet and disease in antiquity, not least among mummies, or the world's oldest _____ [fill in the blank]).

Absent from the range of popular writing in archaeology mentioned so far is the extended essay, written for a non-professional and non-specialized readership. Examples of such essays in archaeology are rather rare – which may be one reason, among others (including size of potential readership, and thus sales), why there is not an archaeological equivalent of the annually-appearing anthologies such as *Best Science Writing, Best Food Writing*, or *Best American Travel Writing*. The essay form involves detailed engagement with an *argument*, over the course of several thousand words, in which the quality and power of the writing itself is paramount. Neither of the two most recent guides to effective writing in archaeology – Brian Fagan's *Writing Archeology: Telling Stories about the Past* (2006), and Graham Connah's *Writing about Archaeology* (2010) – really focus on this form of composition. As will be clear from what follows (and Ch. 2), some of the best examples of writing in English in this genre have appeared in *The New Yorker*, although other interesting examples may be found on-line (e.g., Verini 2015).

Writing for the People in Other Disciplines

While it is possible to find excellent books and articles about archaeology written for a non-specialized audience, they remain relatively few compared to those produced by scholars in other disciplines and they generally reach much smaller groups of people. By contrast to what happens in archaeology, books and articles about the sciences and the history of science regularly appeal to large and diverse audiences. Neither of the editors of this book is specially interested in oncology, or evolutionary biology, or the history of geology, and yet we both have derived learning and pleasure from the writings of authors such as Siddhartha Mukherjee, Stephen Jay Gould, and Martin J. S. Rudwick. Although these scholars are (or were) involved in highly specialized fields of research, we and many of their readers have been captivated and delighted by their powerful, engaging prose – even when that prose deals with malignant white blood cells, or single-celled marine creatures, or Victorian mastodons. And so it seemed to us worth asking: How have they succeeded in communicating the achievements and challenges of their own scientific and scholarly endeavors to a non-specialized audience? There is no single formula, but we have identified a few salient points that may help us reflect on how to produce better and more widely accessible writing about archaeology.

First and most importantly, archaeologists must become aware of the need and virtues of engaging with people other than archaeologists. Many specialists in the sciences have felt the urge to traverse the distance separating a non-specialized audience from the complexities of a major scientific problem or debate. For example, Mukherjee, an oncologist by training, was compelled to bridge that divide when one of his patients, a woman with stomach cancer, said to him: "I'm willing to go on fighting, but I need to know what it is that I'm battling" (McGrath 2010). Because Mukherjee was not capable of answering his patient's question or pointing her to a book that could explain what cancer was, he decided to write "a biography of cancer" – *The Emperor of All Maladies* (2010). Unlike cancer, archaeology will rarely be a matter of life or death, but it is an eminently social activity involving many different stakeholders. Specialists and non-specialists alike stand to learn and be inspired by the conversation, just as Mukherjee acknowledges he was by interaction with his patients.

One particularly important group of non-specialized interlocutors is students – not primarily graduate students or those who are already sold on archaeology, but rather young undergraduates, most of whom will not become professionals in our field, but who may nevertheless develop strong avocational or personal interests in it. Interaction with students has moved scholars in other disciplines to write books and articles that are both learned and widely accessible. For example, Rudwick, a historian of earth sciences, became aware of the necessity to produce writing for non-specialists when he was planning a series of lectures on the history of paleontology and he "discovered the unreliability of the most obvious 'secondary' works when matched against a reading of the primary sources" (Rudwick 1972). The challenge of explaining the history and principles of our own discipline to a general audience has an often unforeseen, but valuable side-effect: it can expose some of our preconceptions, biases, and shortcomings. Part of our duty as archaeologists is to engage in dialogue with people other than professional practitioners – and this not simply in order to do fundraising or as a token of gratitude, but because we ourselves should understand, promote, and question the relevance and reach of our own discipline. What better place to do that than in front of classes of eager and curious, but skeptical and questioning students?

Like any specialized field of research, contemporary archaeology can be complex and hyper-technical. Rather than avoid specific detail or difficult concepts when writing for non-specialists – as is done in many English-language archaeology magazines, such as most of those mentioned above – we could try to emulate writers in the sciences who have managed to capture the excitement and challenges of their own disciplines, while avoiding some of the forbidding specificity and technical language they must use when communicating with colleagues. In an obituary published the day after Stephen Jay Gould died, his colleague and sometimes collaborator, the evolutionary biologist Richard Lewontin, explained why Gould was exceptional:

> He was the best science writer for the public when it came to explaining evolution. Steve did not try to make it simple; he tried and succeeded in explaining the complications. He made readers appreciate how messy and variable life is. Rather than being a popularizer of science, Steve always told the truth in ways people could understand, and he did it better than anyone.
>
> [*Harvard University Gazette* 2002]

Gould was a master of analogy and surprising juxtapositions, as demonstrated in nearly all of his monthly columns written for *Natural History* magazine between 1974 and 2001, reprinted as collected essays in a series of ten books, themselves with arresting titles – *The Flamingo's Smile* (1985), *Bully for Brontosaurus* (1991), *Leonardo's Mountain of Clams and the Diet of Worms* (1998), and so on. Whose curiosity would not be piqued when faced with articles entitled "Phyletic Size Decrease in Hershey Bars" (in Gould 1983) or "The Spandrels of San Marco and the Panglossian Paradigm" (Gould and Lewontin 1979)? Both are articles of utmost seriousness, yet the former is a popular essay and the latter a contribution to the most learned of scientific journals. Who knows how many hours each month it took Gould to write his essays, which are at once so engaging, witty, and deeply learned? He was able, though, simultaneously to live the life of a Harvard professor in evolutionary biology, conducting research and writing academic monographs for his professional colleagues. To be able to write so effectively in both registers, as it were, is undoubtedly a very rare gift; but that does not mean that more of us should not aspire to do so.

Still, there are infinite ways of tackling complexity. In *The Emperor of All Maladies*, for example, Mukherjee tells the life-story of an illness that has existed for thousands of years. The rhetorical maneuver of treating cancer almost anthropomorphically, as if it had a mind and a personality of its own, allowed him to ground massive amounts of technical and historical knowledge in vivid detail. In fact, Mukherjee did so in such a way that a reader understands not only the devastating effects that cancer can have on people, and the historical struggle to make sense of an elusive, shape-shifting disease, but also what it is like to be at the forefront of actually doing cancer research.

Finally, Mukherjee, Gould, and Rudwick clearly enjoy reading and writing. Which leads us to a troubling paradox: those of us who are professional teachers of archaeology realize that it is primarily through writing that we are gauged by our peers and that we gauge our students. Books, articles, dissertations, term papers, cover letters, recommendation letters: at least for the foreseeable future, prose will continue to be our primary medium of communication. And yet we are prisoners of our prose, because there is so little explicit reflection about writing in the classroom or in faculty discussion or even in specialized journals. It is shocking that we do not think more about writing, about how to craft an argument, about the importance of word choices or punctuation, nor about the use of metaphor, the abuse of jargon, or the inanity of certain currently hot keywords. It is just assumed that people will eventually figure out how to write about archaeology. Only rarely, for example, do we ask Ph.D. students in our departments to write without the shield of a scholarly apparatus. And yet, if the shield is removed, so too is a straitjacket. Powerful authors on archaeological matters, from Herodotus to Mary Beard, are gripping because of the obvious delight they derive from writing. One of the great joys of archaeology is that the discipline demands creativity, originality, and risk-taking – not because we regularly have to face aliens or cannibals or Nazis à la Indiana Jones, but because the blank page is totally uncharted territory.

Beyond all this, there is an additional reason why exemplars such as Mukherjee, Gould, and Rudwick are so necessary to consider in the case of archaeological writing: they consistently set the bar high and never underestimate the reader. The editor-in-chief of *Archaeology* magazine for 23 years, Peter A. Young, recently contributed some reflections on archaeological writing to a book entitled *Archaeology in Society: Its Relevance in the Modern World* (Rockman and Flatman 2012). The title says it all: "In Praise of the Storytellers" (Young 2012). Young's piece conceives of archaeological writing for a popular publication entirely in terms of *stories* – scholars sharing their evocative personal tales, conveying the thrill and excitement of what they do, expressing their emotional involvement with the past that drives archaeological discovery. Brian Fagan takes much the same line in his book *Writing Archaeology: Telling Stories about the Past* (2006), whose first chapter, entitled "Come, Let Me Tell You a Tale," rams home the point with "Rule 1: Always Tell a Story." To us, however, this seems all too often like pandering to the crowd. Steven J. Gould's masterful essays rarely, if ever, took the form of neatly crafted narratives of discovery, let alone stories hyped up by the injection of a highly personal angle or the breathless exhilaration of field research. His success – and that of other similar writers – came not from simplifying ("dumbing down") or assuming that the message must be reduced to a story-line. It came rather from *embracing* complexity, messiness, and open-endedness, and yet writing in crystal-clear prose illuminated by arresting analogies and captivating word-sketches.

The Archaeology for the People Competition

This, then, was the general context that led us to conceive the idea of organizing a competition, open to all-comers, to submit an extended essay on any archaeological topic written in a compelling style that held the possibility of engaging the interest of any reader, irrespective of background. In the USA, National Public Radio has promoted the idea of "driveway moments" – reports so fascinatingly told that, even though one has arrived home from work, one cannot bear to switch off the radio and get out of the car before hearing the end of the piece. In a comparable vein, articles in magazines such as *Cabinet* or *Granta* feature powerful writing, with minimal visual illustration and zero or little scholarly apparatus (i.e., no subtitles, no footnotes, no bibliography), that have the ability to draw the reader, ineluctably, into extended accounts of topics in which he or she had no prior reason to be interested. From time to time, these and other magazines publish articles on archaeological subjects, and we felt that Elif Batuman's 2011 *New Yorker* essay on the wider issues raised by the new discoveries at the site of Göbekli Tepe in eastern Turkey (see Ch. 2) served as an admirable model for the kind of gripping prose we hoped to elicit via our competition.

And so we drew up rules. Our competition would be open to anyone, worldwide, except those directly associated with the Joukowsky Institute. It would place the emphasis on strong prose by limiting illustrative material to a single, arresting figure (as is generally the case with *New Yorker* articles). We offered a substantial cash prize of $5,000 for the winning essay, in order to encourage participation. Here is the call for submissions, circulated in December 2013:

Archaeology for the People:

The Joukowsky Institute Competition for Accessible Archaeological Writing

As archaeologists, we write for each other in journal articles, book chapters, monographs, and other forums, using language that makes sense to fellow members of the profession. That is as it should be: we have no more reason to "dumb down" our findings than do, say, astronomers, brain surgeons, or epidemiologists in publications for their own communities of scholarship. At the same time, the results of archaeological discovery and analysis are important and deserve the widest possible audience: archaeology has momentous findings to report, and for the periods before written history stands as the only source of evidence we have for the human condition.

Unlike other fields which have benefited from brilliant writing in a popular vein by scholars such as Stephen Jay Gould or Carl Sagan, archaeology as a discipline has done rather poorly at the effective communication of its most interesting and important results to the general public, and indeed to itself, which is also important. Certainly, some writers, such as Brian Fagan, have excelled at the task of popular dissemination of some of archaeology's big themes. Yet most websites, TV shows, and archaeology magazines (such as *Archaeology* or *Biblical Archaeology Review*) tend to emphasize the sheer luck of discovery, the romance of archaeology, and supposed "mysteries" that archaeology tries (but usually has failed) to resolve.

We believe that archaeology is worthy of a better level of writing, one that is accessible and exciting to non-specialists, but at the same time avoids excessive simplification, speculation, mystification, or romanticization. As a discipline, we have some fascinating and astonishing results to report, findings that impact our entire understanding of who we are as a species, and how we have come to be as we are now. Some of the most effective writing in this vein has appeared not in professional venues, but in publications with a far wider readership. As just one example, we would cite Elif Batuman's article in *The New Yorker Magazine* (December 19, 2011) on the Göbekli Tepe site in Turkey, and the many fundamental questions it raises about religion, technology, and human social evolution.

With these thoughts in mind, and to encourage more writing in this vein, we propose a competition for new archaeological writing. We invite the submission of accessible and engaging articles, accompanied by a single illustration, that showcase any aspect of archaeology of potential interest to a wide readership. As an incentive, we offer **a prize of $5,000** to the winner. The prize-winning article, together with those by eight to ten other runners-up, will be published in 2015 in a volume of the *Joukowsky Institute Publication* series (published and distributed by Oxbow Books).

Rules

1. Anyone may enter the competition, except faculty, postdoctoral fellows, and students at the Joukowsky Institute for Archaeology and the Ancient World, Brown University.
2. Authors must be able to vouch that their article is solely their own work and has not been published elsewhere.
3. Articles should be about five to six thousand words in length; include no references, notes, or other scholarly apparatus; be accompanied by a single piece of artwork; and be submitted as a double-spaced Word document. The first page should provide your name, address, and e-mail.
4. The deadline for receipt of entries is September 1, 2014. Articles must be submitted electronically, to joukowsky_institute@brown.edu
5. Submissions with be read anonymously and adjudicated by a panel consisting of faculty and postdoctoral fellows at Brown University.
6. The result of the competition will be announced by November 2014.
7. Questions concerning the competition should be directed to Prof. John Cherry (john_cherry@brown.edu) and Prof. Felipe Rojas (felipe_rojas@brown.edu).

This call for entries was circulated widely, although chiefly within archaeological circles. For example, it was sent out to most departments of archaeology in the USA, Europe, and Australasia; it was posted to wide-circulation listservs, such as *AegeaNet* and *Agade*; it reached the very large online membership of the World Archaeology Congress; and it was drawn to the attention of the 35,000 or so students who had signed up for the "Archaeology's Dirty Little Secrets" MOOC (Ch. 10). In the event, we did not find an effective way to draw attention to the competition among non-archaeological constituencies – such as, for example, students of journalism or non-fiction writing – and this undoubtedly restricted the range of types of essays received. Although we initially thought about contacting literary and cultural journals (such as the *Times Literary Supplement* or *The London Review of Books*) as well as journalism and creative literature departments, we encountered two obstacles. Prices for advertising were prohibitive in the former, and we found no effective way of accessing the latter. (If we embark on a second iteration of this competition, outreach to non-archaeologists who may be interested in writing will be a major priority).

By the time the competition closed in September 2014, we had received about 150 entries from participants in more than two dozen countries. Unsurprisingly, since the competition was conducted in English, the majority of entrants were from the USA, the UK, the countries of the British Commonwealth, and other parts of the world where English is the common tongue. But entries were also received from a wide array of other nations: for example, in Europe (France, the Netherlands, Italy, Germany, Spain, Portugal, Slovenia, Greece); in South America (Colombia, Brazil, Argentina, Chile); and in East Asia (Singapore, Hong Kong, Malaysia, Nepal).

The submitted essays were read blind (i.e., without identifying information about the author) by a panel of 14 readers, drawn mainly from the faculty and postdoctoral fellows of the Joukowsky Institute, with additional assistance from Brown faculty in the Department of Anthropology, the Haffenreffer Museum of Anthropology, and the John Nicholas Brown Center for Public Humanities and Cultural Heritage. The judges' remit was to select essays that they found exciting and engaging and, most of all, that they enjoyed reading. The result was a winning essay (published here as Ch. 3, "An Archaeology of Sustenance: The Endangered Market Gardens of Istanbul," by Chantel White, Aleksandar Shopov, and Marta Ostovich), and five additional submissions deemed by the judges to be meritorious runners-up (Chs. 4–8). We are very pleased to showcase the work of these authors in this *JIP* volume.

Pushback

Yet, somewhat to our surprise, we received reactions, sometimes negative, to our competition from several provocative directions. They are worth mentioning here for the underlying assumptions they reveal about effective writing in archaeology, as well as for their suggestions of possibilities for future initiatives.

There were those, for example, who objected to the fact that the competition was restricted to essays written in English. One e-mail correspondent (in fact, one of those who subsequently contributed to the Questionnaire of Ch. 11) wrote:

> This seems a very worthwhile initiative – provided English is your mother tongue. Translation or language editing appears to be against the rules... Should competitions on a global level not offer equal opportunities, whatever your native language might be? Do we need accessible writing in English more than in other languages? To me, this competition, although well intended, leaves an unpleasant aftertaste.

Our intention, of course, was not to be colonialist or exclusionary, nor insensitive to non-English speakers, but merely realistic about the impracticality of adjudicating entries in multiple languages. Would we have to commission translations? Or find native speakers in many languages to assist us? That might just be possible for languages such as French, German, Italian, Spanish, Portuguese, Russian, or Arabic. But what would we do if we received submissions written in Pashto, or Nahuatl, or Tagalog? Even if we could surmount the logistics of such linguistic challenges, the translations would likely miss the nuances and subtleties of the original, and become as much the work of the translator as the author – *traduttore, traditore*. Like it or not, at least for the moment, English is a *lingua franca*.

The competition also attracted some discussion and critique on the blog sites of the World Archaeological Congress and the Deutsche Gesellschaft für Ur- und Frühgeschichte (German Society for Pre- and Protohistory). A correspondent to the latter, for example, complained that the competition was fundamentally flawed, since its entire conception and formulation was limited to the academic ivory tower, thus entirely missing the audience we professed to be trying to reach. Limiting the judging panel to faculty and postdoctoral fellows in archaeology – rather than including, for example, "a bored, pubescent teenager" – meant that the competition was doomed from the outset. This same critic lamented the apparent restriction against submissions in the form of poems or fantasy stories (not entirely true, under the rules, although certainly not what we primarily had in mind), and regretted the fact that the best essays would be published in an "unknown publication series" of the Joukowsky Institute! We were not after archaeological poems or imaginative prose that had a leading archaeologist, say Ian Hodder or Cyprian Broodbank, imagined as a character in *Game of*

Thrones. Our ambitions were much more modest: we wanted people to write about archaeology in English prose much in the way that – to add examples beyond those already cited – Peter Gallison has written about relativity or Atul Gawande about the challenges of dealing with phantom limb syndrome.

Another line of attack came from those who believe that we all live in the post-print era – that the best, most current, and most readable content on archaeology is to be found online, published as it happens, creating an instant connection with an interested, global audience. As one correspondent put it:

> My concern is that pieces that I have written (and that my colleagues have written) have all appeared on archaeology blogs. We find that most archaeological writing (including serious archaeological writing) is done on online spaces, publicly. Would it be possible for entrants to submit links to a post (or posts) of their archaeological writing, pieces that often include images and links to related media, things that do not necessarily translate well to print? Would you consider collections of public archaeology writing, or platforms that host serious archaeology writing intended to engage and inform the public?

This correspondent went on to cite a number of archaeology blogs he felt offered good examples of thoughtful writing on archaeology for a public audience. We do not disagree, although our competition was targeted at well-constructed, publishable essays of far greater length than most blog posts. Blogs often tend to be hastily written, partisan, and ephemeral. But this, certainly, is something to consider for future iterations of a competition such as ours.

Finally, of all the queries we received from potential contestants, the most frequent concerned our strict instruction that the essay be accompanied by just a single piece of artwork. Our model here was that of a *New Yorker* essay or *Cabinet* piece, which in most cases is accompanied by only one image, generally printed opposite the title page, and intended to be intriguing and suggestive, rather than factually illustrative, in a journalistic sense. This turned out to be a limitation that many contestants, no doubt more familiar with the traditional canons of archaeological publication, found tough to deal with. Some, in fact, wrote to us to express the view that, in imposing this restriction, we were cutting off our own nose to spite our face. Archaeology is a field that is tactile, tangible, hands-on, they said: all about objects, artifacts, things – witness the titles of two very recent books in the field, Ian Hodder's *Entangled: An Archaeology of the Relationships between Humans and Things* (2012), and Bjørnar Olsen *et al.*'s *Archaeology: The Discipline of Things* (2012). Why would we want to limit essays in this way, by insisting that they be primarily about the writing rather than the images?

Pictures That Should Talk

Our answer to that question is that we are dealing here with two different types of discourse. The *Archaeology for the People* competition was explicitly designed to elicit powerful, engaging, arresting prose about archaeology – a discourse whose power arises from *words*, not imagery.

Handbooks such as *Writing about Archaeology* (Connah 2010: 91–135) invariably include a chapter on "Visual Explanation," which emphasizes the importance of effective illustration in almost any book or article. Well-conceived maps and plans; clear, even striking, illustrations of sites and artifacts; great photographs – these are of course an integral element of all good professional publications. This is not quite the same thing, however, as a photo-essay, which attempts to provide an archeological account in purely visual terms, with little verbal description. Such accounts can be very powerful, precisely because they are so evocative. Our models here are the kinds of photo-essays that have been published, for decades, every quarter in *Granta* magazine: lots of photos, but often little by way of description, explanation, or comment, leaving a great deal to the viewer's imagination. Typically, they boast minimal introductory prose, just enough to situate the images that follow, not more than necessary to let the photos resonate and speak for themselves.

Ch. 9 provides an example of such a way of proceeding. Laurel Bestock's project takes place on a very remote island (Uronarti) in the Nile in the northern Sudan, hours from the nearest town. Doing archaeology in such a setting is clearly exhilarating (bathing near Nile crocodiles!), yet involves some severe privations and demands a good deal of improvisation. Simply feeding a small archaeological field crew in such a setting poses major challenges. Bestock's beautiful photographs, extracted from a longer work in preparation, capture the realities and logistics of fieldwork in a way that a purely verbal description would be much less capable of doing. Although eventually she will produce an account for her academic colleagues of the outcome of this field research, meanwhile images alone can provide a sense of the practicalities involved in wresting data from such a far-flung research location.

A Questionnaire to Define Archaeology for the People

The final chapter of this book represents the outcome of what was, admittedly, a relatively last-minute idea, but one that in the event proved to be fruitful. As we formulated the aims and rules of the *Archaeology for the People* competition, and, subsequently, read our way through the more than three

quarters of a million words of the submitted essays and discussed our reactions
to them, we were constantly forced to think about and articulate our own
views concerning what good archaeological writing would look like. We also
continued to ponder some of the questions that had set the competition in
motion in the first place. What examples exist of archaeological writing that
succeeds in reaching a non-specialized audience, and how was it achieved?
Why has archaeology spawned so few distinguished popularizers, compared
to many other fields? Have the demands and opportunities of alternative
media overrun traditional printed publications? Who is our audience, and
why should it matter to bring archaeology to that body?

    And so, we thought, why not ask a small group of archaeological writers
for their responses to these questions? All but one of the eight people
we approached are archaeologists (the one exception being a professional
author; we would gladly have included more views from non-archaeologists,
had we known of more good examples of effective archaeological writers).
The individuals in Chapter 11 have distinguished themselves either by
publishing powerful, engaging, accessible books on archaeological topics; or
by presenting archaeology on television; or by writing in strong terms about
their visions of what archaeology is, or could be, or should be. We have
chosen to present their various answers to each question side-by-side, and in a
scrambled order (Ch. 11). Needless to say, the responses are very varied – not
in the sense of being mutually contradictory, but rather in terms of the very
different directions from which they approach the basic questions we asked of
them. That is as it should be: in seeking to do a better job of explaining to a
broad public why archaeology matters, and why it is so endlessly fascinating,
we need all the ideas we can muster.

The Sanctuary:
The World's Oldest Temple and the Dawn of Civilization

Elif Batuman

View of the excavation trenches at Göbekli Tepe with many exposed monoliths.
(Photo by Müge Durusu-Tanrıöver)

Editorial note: *This article first appeared in the December 19, 2011 issue of* The New Yorker. *As discussed in Ch. 1, it was singled out as a fine example of the type of writing we hoped to solicit via the* Archaeology for the People *essay competition. It is reprinted here by kind permission of the author, who owns all distribution rights.*

L ate one October evening, I flew into Urfa, the city believed by Turkish
   Muslims to be the Ur of the Chaldeans, the birthplace of the prophet
Abraham. My hotel had clearly been designed for pilgrims. A door in the
lobby led to a men-only steam bath. There was no women's bath. In my room,
a sign indicating the direction of prayer was posted over the nonalcoholic
minibar. Directly outside the window, Vegas-style lights stretching across the
main drag spelled, in two-foot-high letters, "WELCOME TO THE CITY
OF PROPHETS."

Urfa is in southeastern Anatolia, about thirty miles north of the Syrian
border. Tens of thousands of people come here every year to visit a cave where
Abraham may have been born and a fishpond marking the site of the pyre
where he was almost burned up by Nimrod, except that God transformed
the fire into water and the coals into fish. According to another local legend,
God sent a swarm of mosquitos to torment Nimrod, and a mosquito flew up
Nimrod's nose and started chewing on his brain. Nimrod ordered his men to
beat his head with wooden mallets, shouting, "*Vur ha, vur ha!*" ("Hit me, hit
me!"), and that's how his city came to be called Urfa. Urfa also has a Greek
name, Edessa, under which it is enshrined in the Eastern Orthodox Church
as the origin of perhaps the world's first icon: a handkerchief on which Jesus
wiped his face, preserving his image. (Known as the Image of Edessa, the
holy handkerchief was said to be a gift from Christ to King Abgar V, who
was suffering from leprosy.) In 1984, Urfa was officially renamed Şanlıurfa –
"glorious Urfa" – in honor of its resistance against the Allied Forces during the
Turkish War of Independence. Most people still call it Urfa. The city's religious
sites also include the cave where Job is said to have suffered through his boils.

I, too, was in town on a pilgrimage, visiting a site that predates Abraham
and Job and monotheism by some eight millennia: a vast complex of
Stonehenge-style megalithic circles in the Urfa countryside. For thousands
of years, this Early Neolithic structure lay buried under multiple strata of
prehistoric trash, and therefore just looked like a big hill. Its Turkish name
is Göbekli Tepe: "hill with a potbelly," or "fat hill."

There are a number of unsettling things about Göbekli Tepe. It's estimated
to be eleven thousand years old – six and a half thousand years older than the
Great Pyramid, five and a half thousand years older than the earliest known
cuneiform texts, and about a thousand years older than the walls of Jericho,
formerly believed to be the world's most ancient monumental structure. The site
comprises more than sixty multi-ton T-shaped limestone pillars, most of them
engraved with bas-reliefs of dangerous animals: not the docile, edible bison
and deer featured in Paleolithic cave paintings but ominous configurations of
lions, foxes, boars, vultures, scorpions, spiders, and snakes. The site has yielded
no traces of habitation – no trash pits, no water source, no houses, no hearths,

no roofs, no domestic plant or animal remains – and is therefore believed to have been built by hunter-gatherers, who used it as a religious sanctuary. Comparisons of iconography from similar sites indicate that different groups congregated there from up to sixty miles away. Mysteriously, the pillars appear to have been buried, deliberately and all at once, around 8200 B.C., some thirteen hundred years after their construction.

The idea of a religious monument built by hunter-gatherers contradicts most of what we thought we knew about religious monuments and about hunter-gatherers. Hunter-gatherers are traditionally believed to have lacked complex symbolic systems, social hierarchies, and the division of labor, three things you probably need before you can build a twenty-two-acre megalithic temple. Formal religion, meanwhile, is supposed to have appeared only after agriculture produced such hierarchical social relations as required a cosmic backstory to keep them going and supplied a template for the power relationship between gods and mortals. The findings at Göbekli Tepe suggest that we have the story backward – that it was actually the need to build a sacred site that first obliged hunter-gatherers to organize themselves as a workforce, to spend long periods of time in one place, to secure a stable food supply, and eventually to invent agriculture.

I got a ride to Göbekli Tepe from an overweight, truculent taxi-driver, a friend of the hotel receptionist. We left the city via a giant traffic circle. Drivers were entering and exiting this diabolical wheel from all directions, switching lanes and cutting each other off, without using their turn signals or altering their speed. Where a non-Urfa driver might speed up or slow down, it seemed, an Urfa driver preferred simply to honk his horn. Horn-honking had become a symbolic rite, evoking the function once filled, in the world of physical reality, by use of the brake pedal.

The traffic circle eventually disgorged us onto the rural highway to Mardin, the home town of the world's tallest man, an eight-foot-three-inch-tall farmer with pituitary gigantism. We drove past numerous dealers in firearms and agricultural machinery, making visible the primeval oscillation between hunting and farming. Exiting onto a dirt road, which wound for several miles through the hills, we ended up in a dusty lot, where a couple of minivans were parked next to an informational tableau. Two tethered camels gazed at the plains with droopy, self-satisfied expressions.

I walked past the camels and up a slope, and came to a group of graduate students crouched on boulders, hunched over a drumlike sieve full of dirt, which was suspended by cables from a makeshift wooden tripod. They looked as if they were trying to invent fire. I asked what they were doing. A round-faced young man wearing glasses and a panama hat glanced up, with a tight, conversation-ending smile. "Sifting dirt," he replied, intensifying his smile and turning his back.

I climbed up the hill, toward the solitary mulberry tree that stands at its summit. Tattered strips of cloth tied to the branches testify to its former use by local farmers as a "wishing tree." The pillars came into view, as unfamiliar and unexpected as an extraterrestrial settlement. One face of the hill had been almost completely excavated, exposing four stone circles, each made up of a dozen or so pillars with two larger pillars in the middle. Several of these megaliths had surprisingly poor foundations, and were now standing thanks only to wooden supports. Archeologists speculate that the weak foundations may have had some acoustic purpose: perhaps the pillars were meant to hum in the wind.

During their centuries of use, the pillars were periodically buried, with new pillars built on top of or alongside the old ones. The circles thus stand at different depths in the hill, and have been connected by various wooden scaffolds, ladders, and walkways. Jens Notroff, the graduate student with whom I had coordinated my visit, took me on a tour. It was an immensely destabilizing landscape. Everywhere you looked, you saw something that wasn't supposed to exist. Hunter-gatherers, for example, weren't supposed to make larger-than-life human representations, which are a violation of a purely animistic, nonhierarchic world view. And yet, as Notroff pointed out, the pillars are almost certainly humanoid figures, with long narrow bodies and large oblong heads. There are pillars depicted with clasped hands, or wearing foxtail loincloths. One is wearing a necklace with a bucranium, or bull's head. If the pillars represent specific individuals, the bull might be a form of identification, a name, like Sitting Bull.

Because the bas-reliefs of Göbekli Tepe, unlike the cave paintings of the Upper Paleolithic, offer no picture of daily life – no hunting scenes, and very few of the aurochs, gazelles, and deer that made up most of the hunter-gatherer diet – they are believed to be symbols, a message we don't know how to read. The animals might be mythical characters, symbolic scapegoats, tribal families, mnemonic devices, or perhaps totemic scarecrows, guarding the pillars from evil. They include a scorpion the size of a small suitcase, and a jackal-like creature with an exposed rib cage. On one pillar, a row of lumpy, eyeless "ducks" float above an extremely convincing boar, with an erect penis. Another relief consists of the simple contour of a fox, like a chalk outline at a murder scene, also with a distinct penis. So far, all the mammals represented at Göbekli Tepe are visibly male, with the exception of one fox, which, in place of a penis, has several snakes coming out of its abdomen. Perhaps the most debated composition portrays a vulture carrying a round object on one wing; below its feet, a headless male torso displays yet another erect penis. On an informational board near the vulture, the German and English texts mention the erect penis; the Turkish text does not. I like to think that, when it comes to identifying a headless man with an erection, I'm as sharp-eyed as the next person, but I wouldn't have recognized this one without assistance. To me, he looked more like a samovar.

The images don't seem to share a unifying style, or even a standard level of draftsmanship. Some are stylized and geometric, others remarkably lifelike. "They can do naturalistic representations," Notroff said. "So when they don't do it, it's a choice." He told me about a statue of a man which was believed to be eleven thousand years old: the oldest known life-sized human sculpture. Discovered in the nineteen-nineties in downtown Urfa, the Urfa Man now resides in a glass case in the Şanlıurfa Museum, where I visited him that afternoon. Mouthless, carved from pale limestone, with obsidian eyes in sunken sockets and hands clasped to his groin, he resembled a wasted snowman.

I spent the next few days at the site. Over the course of several trips, the receptionist's surly taxi-driver friend dropped his guard a bit. We discussed Urfa traffic. When I remarked that I had yet to see a woman behind the wheel of a car, he assured me that the number of lady drivers had risen "by at least seventy per cent" in recent years. Another day, when we got to Göbekli Tepe, he offered to write me a receipt for double the actual fare, so that I could cheat my employers.

Excavation began at six-thirty every morning, when there was still pink light in the sky and a chill in the air. On the scene were forty Kurdish workers, twenty German and Turkish archaeology students, and an official from the Izmir museum of archaeology, who had been appointed by the Turkish Ministry of Culture and Tourism to keep tabs on progress and to insure that the ruins were being made accessible to the two hundred or so tourists who turned up every day. Many of these visitors became angry and frustrated at not being allowed into the trench to see the pillars, so workers were building them a boardwalk.

Excavation was under way on a new trench, on the other side of a low limestone ridge. The area had been dug up in squares, varying in depth between three and seven feet. Seen from above, they resembled rooms in a doll house. In one square, students were measuring the depth of the layers of backfill; in another, three workers, their heads swathed in purple cloths, hoisted a boulder into a wheelbarrow. One of the center squares contained a newly discovered pillar with the most intricate bas-reliefs to date: rows of sinuous-necked cranes and snakes packed efficiently together, like sardines in a can.

The workers digging the trenches had learned to set aside objects of potential archeological interest. One day, they found an irregularly shaped stone, about the size of a tea tray, its upper surface pitted with small hemispherical holes. "We believe it was cultic," one graduate student told me of this object. "That's what we say whenever we don't know the purpose of something. Of course, maybe it was not cultic. Maybe it was a contest, to see who can make the most holes the fastest. Anyway, they didn't have sacred and profane then. It's a young distinction."

In general, it was difficult to engage the graduate students in conversation, either about Neolithic man or about archaeology. The Kurdish workers, however, loved to talk. One day, a few of them started looking through my copy of a monograph on Göbekli Tepe. They reminisced about the order in which the reliefs in the photographs had been discovered, who had been there and who hadn't. They made fun of one of their friends who had been photographed with an enormous black beard. He had shaved off his beard a long time ago, and they all thought he looked better now.

The workers spanned several generations, from mustached grandfathers in baggy pants, with cigarettes clenched in the corners of their mouths, to jeans-wearing youths with fabulous hair. Their village, I learned, was called Örencik. Some people called it by an older name, Karaharabe, which means "black ruin." Nobody seemed to know where the black ruin was. They told me about the hazards of the job, which included having a snake jump out at you from between the rocks. One day, a worker was bitten by a scorpion and had to be sent to the hospital in a taxi. His friends told me that scorpion bites hurt, but they won't kill you. Snakes are another story. The students found a poisonous snake once, but it was already dead. Someone put it in a bag and took it away.

I asked the workers what it felt like to uncover ten-thousand-year-old reliefs of terrifying animals.

"It's beautiful, actually," one of them said. "It's a beautiful thing. When you first find a pillar, when the top of the stone is just visible – first you ask yourself, What animals will be on it? Then you dig and dig, slowly, bit by bit, because you know that by digging you're causing damage. Slowly, always slowly. But sometimes you can't contain yourself – you think, Let's just quickly look and see what's there." He paused. "Sometimes we wonder, if one of the people from back then were to sit up and talk to us, what would the man say? What language does he speak? What is he? Is he shorter than us or taller than us?"

"That base stone there – it was brought here by human strength!" another worker said. "So we wonder, were the people who carried it much stronger than us? We think the men then were two or three metres tall, and we're only 1.6 or 1.7 metres tall. Of course, we don't actually know anything about it. We're just imagining to ourselves."

In fact, nobody really knows how Neolithic man managed to hew these pillars. Claudia Beuger, an archeologist at the University of Halle, is conducting a study at a limestone quarry in Bavaria, to determine whether she and ten of her students can build a twenty-three-foot Göbekli Tepe-style pillar, using only fire-blasting techniques and basalt "hammers" with no handles. The early results suggest that the job can be completed in ten weeks by either forty-four archaeology students or twenty-two Neolithic people.

The first survey of Göbekli Tepe was begun in 1963, by Peter Benedict, an archeologist from the University of Chicago, who described the site as "a complex of round-topped knolls of red earth," two of which were surmounted by "small cemeteries," probably dating from the Byzantine Empire. It's possible that Benedict, unable to imagine that Neolithic man was capable of producing giant mounds or stone monuments, came across a fragment of carved limestone and mistook it for a medieval tombstone. Nothing about his description made anyone want to rush out and start digging.

The ruins remained sleeping under the earth until the arrival of someone who could recognize them. In 1994, Klaus Schmidt, an archeologist at Heidelberg University, visited the site and immediately understood that Benedict's report had been wrong. He saw that the "knolls" were man-made mounds, and that the flint shards crunching underfoot had been shaped by Neolithic hands. Schmidt had spent much of the previous decade working at Nevalı Çori, a nearby settlement from the ninth millennium B.C., which included both domestic habitations and a "sanctuary" with T-shaped pillars. Nevalı Çori was discovered in 1979 and lost to science in 1992, when it was inundated by the Atatürk Dam and became part of the floor of Lake Atatürk. This left Schmidt in the market for a new Stone Age site. At Göbekli Tepe he saw flints nearly identical to those at Nevalı Çori. When Schmidt saw part of a T-shaped pillar, he recognized that as well. "Within a minute of first seeing it, I knew I had two choices," he has said. "Go away and tell nobody, or spend the rest of my life working here." He went right back to Urfa and bought a house.

The house is a nineteenth-century Ottoman complex, built around a courtyard with a tiled pool. Schmidt lives there with his wife, Çiğdem, also an archeologist, whom he met in Urfa when she was working on another dig. Schmidt, who now works for the German Archeological Institute, says he can't remember a time before he wanted to be an archeologist. As a schoolboy in Bavaria, he learned about the Greeks and the Romans, and thought he would study them when he grew up. Then he found out about Paleolithic cave art, and became determined to find a Bavarian cave with paintings as old and remarkable as the ones in France. He discovered many caves, but no paintings. Because of his interest in caves, he studied geology as well as archaeology, and this is why he could immediately identify Göbekli Tepe as a man-made rather than a natural formation.

Nowadays, Schmidt usually spends the morning at Göbekli Tepe, while Çiğdem works at the house. Schmidt and the students, bearing several large bags of Neolithic detritus, return to Urfa for a late lunch – the Schmidts keep an excellent Turkish cook – and everyone spends the rest of the afternoon at the house, processing the day's finds, which are sorted among various buckets and rectangular sieves in the courtyard. The team's archeozoologist, Joris Peters, introduced me to the variety of animal bones that had been retrieved from the site: leopards, goitered gazelles, wild cattle, wild boar, wild sheep, red deer, Mesopotamian fallow deer, foxes, chukar partridges, cranes, and vultures.

"They were still eating the meat of carnivores," Peters said of the hunter-gatherers, pointing to cut marks on the bones of the foxes. He thinks they may also have eaten the vultures. He showed me the scapula of an aurochs, an extinct forebear of domestic cattle, weighing more than two thousand pounds. Aurochs were eaten at Neolithic feasts, which appear to have been a feature of Göbekli Tepe life. "They were having big parties," Schmidt says. He thinks they might have had beer, even "some kind of drugs."

This was the decadent late stage of Neolithic life. Schmidt characterizes the people of Göbekli Tepe as "the victims of their own success." Their way of life had been so successful that it found material expression in the form of a gigantic stone edifice, a reification of a spiritual world view. The very process of construction changed the world view, making the monument obsolete. Schmidt believes that's why Göbekli Tepe was abandoned: "They did not need it anymore. Now they are farmers and they find new expressions of their religious beliefs."

Schmidt sees no continuity between the Neolithic hunter-gatherers and any more recent culture. At one point, I asked about an Indian astronomer's interpretation of the Göbekli Tepe iconography in terms of the Vedas, which date back to the Bronze Age. Could the bas-relief of the headless man, the vulture, and the round object represent the bird Garuda carrying the sun across the sky? "I wouldn't exclude this possibility, but it's a very, very low probability," Schmidt said. He thinks the scene might illustrate a specifically Neolithic myth involving vultures who carry away the heads of dead people. "Even one thousand years later, nothing is left of this world," he said. "Why should there be anything left six thousand years later?"

An extraordinary thought: The people of Göbekli Tepe weren't wiped out, like other lost civilizations. They simply packed up and went somewhere else – became someone else. It was like the witness-protection program. In a way, they were still all around us. Lots of us were probably descended from them. The more I thought about the headless man the more certain I felt that he was related to me. My father's family comes from Adana, a few hours' drive from Urfa.

The term "Neolithic revolution" was coined in the nineteen-twenties, by the archeologist V. Gordon Childe, to describe the transition from hunting-and-gathering – the dominant mode of subsistence for the two hundred thousand years before the last ice age – to domestication and agriculture. Childe ascribed the shift to climate change, to conditions that dried up the lush forests and plains: humans and animals were drawn together at the last remaining oases, where proximity led to domestication, sedentism, and agriculture. Childe, a disillusioned Stalinist, committed suicide in 1957, soon after the Hungarian Uprising and just as radiocarbon dating was transforming the study of archaeology, but many of his ideas have survived to the present day. Until recently, most archeologists continued to ascribe the Neolithic revolution to a combination of climatic and demographic factors. One notable exception was the late Jacques Cauvin, who, in the seventies, proposed that an early form of religion – a cult of the bull and the fertility goddess – had fostered a fertility-oriented world view that eventually engendered the shift to agriculture.

Schmidt believes that Göbekli Tepe proves Cauvin right – not about the fertility goddess, which seems to be belied by all those erect penises, but about an ideological trigger. He believes that the shift from animism to centralized religion, and from an egalitarian to a hierarchical society, was the cause and not the effect of economic change. Unlike Cauvin, he bases his theory less on the specific symbolic content of Göbekli Tepe, whose meaning remains obscure, than on the simple fact of its existence. Regardless of what the pillars are for, producing them took a lot of man-hours. The workers needed a stable food supply, and the area was rich in wild species like aurochs and einkorn, one of the ancestors of domesticated wheat. Building Göbekli Tepe would also have required some division of labor among overseers, technicians, and workers – another social development that might have precipitated, rather than resulted from, the shift to agriculture.

A surprising fact about the Neolithic revolution is that, according to most evidence, agriculture brought about a steep decline in the standard of living. Studies of Kalahari Bushmen and other nomadic groups show that hunter-gatherers, even in the most inhospitable landscapes, typically spend less than twenty hours a week obtaining food. By contrast, farmers toil from sunup to sundown. Because agriculture relies on the mass cultivation of a handful of starchy crops, a community's whole livelihood can be wiped out overnight by bad weather or pests. Paleontological evidence shows that, compared with hunter-gatherers, early farmers had more anemia and vitamin deficiencies, died younger, had worse teeth, were more prone to spinal deformity, and caught more infectious diseases, as a result of living close to other humans and to livestock. A study of skeletons in Greece and Turkey found that the average height of humans dropped six inches between the end of the ice age and 3000 B.C.; modern Greeks and Turks still haven't regained the height of their hunter-gatherer ancestors. That Kurdish worker at Göbekli Tepe was right: Neolithic man probably *was* taller than him.

Why would anyone stick with such a miserable way of life? Jared Diamond, the author of "Guns, Germs, and Steel," describes the situation as a classic bait-and-switch. Hunter-gatherers were "seduced by the transient abundance they enjoyed until population growth caught up with increased food production." By then they were locked in – they had to farm more and more land just to keep everyone alive. Deriving strength from their large, poorly nourished numbers, the farmers gradually killed off most of the hunter-gatherers and drove the rest from their land. Diamond considers agriculture to be not just a setback but "the worst mistake in the history of the human race," the origin of "the gross social and sexual inequality, the disease and despotism, that curse our existence."

Was the Neolithic revolution really a "curse" on our existence? The high emotional and political stakes of this question were manifested in a cover article in *Der Spiegel* in 2006, which proposed Göbekli Tepe as the historical site of the Garden of Eden. The Turkish press enthusiastically picked up the story. Given their preexisting claim to Job and Abraham, some locals reasoned, it would actually have been remarkable if Adam and Eve *hadn't* been from Urfa. Evidence for the identification with Eden included Göbekli Tepe's position between the Tigris and the Euphrates, the copious snake imagery, and Schmidt's characterization of the region as "a paradise for hunter-gatherers." But the theory really draws its power from a reading of the Fall as an allegory for the shift from hunting-and-gathering to farming. In Eden, man and woman lived as companions, unashamed of their nakedness, surrounded by friendly animals and by "trees that were pleasing to the eye and good for food." The fruit of the Tree of Knowledge, like the first fruits of cultivation, brought on an immediate, irrevocable curse. Man now had to work the earth, to eat of it all the days of his life. According to Maimonides, there are legends in which Adam, after the Fall, went on to write "several works about agriculture."

God's terrible words to Eve – "I will greatly increase your pains in childbearing; in pain you will give birth to children. Your desire will be for your husband, and he will rule over you" – may refer to a decline in women's health and status produced, in early agricultural societies, by the economic need to have children who would till and inherit the land. Women, having access to goat's milk and cereal, may have weaned their children earlier, resulting in more frequent, more debilitating pregnancies. The institution of private property, meanwhile, made paternal certainty a vital concern, and monogamy, particularly for women, was strictly enforced.

To continue the interpretation, the story of Cain and Abel may be taken as an illustration of the zero-sum game of primogeniture, as well as an allegory for the slaughter of nomadic pasturage by urban agriculture. Having killed his brother, Cain goes on to found the world's first city and name it after his son Enoch. Read in this spirit, large chunks of the Old Testament – the territorial feuds, the constant threat of exile or extinction, the sexual jealousy and sibling rivalry – begin to resemble the handbook for a grim new scarcity economy of land and love.

What's at issue in the Garden of Eden allegory is whether agriculture was a qualitative break in human history – "a catastrophe," as Diamond puts it, "from which we have never recovered." Was the human condition ever fundamentally different from the way it is now? Might the past three thousand years not be the last word on who we are? Whole world views ride on the answers to these questions. Friedrich Engels, for example, believed that prehistoric man had once lived under a classless "primitive communism," and that monogamy was invented by greedy men, so that their sons could get their hoarded wealth after they died. Engels needed to believe in a time when the Communist utopia had been, and could again be, reconciled with human nature. Darwin, by contrast, maintained that, even if humans had once been polygamous, they had never lived in sexual freedom: male jealousy had always led to "the inculcation of female virtue." (Jealousy was interpreted by later Darwinians to reflect the male's desire to restrict paternal investment to his own genetic offspring.) This view, implying that the premium placed on female chastity was one of the ground rules of life on earth, accorded both with Victorian mores and with Darwin's view of the organism as a machine for insuring the survival of individual traits. Freud, meanwhile, believed that the nuclear family was universal, and that the "primeval family," riven by the Oedipus complex, had been even more repressive than haute-bourgeois Vienna. The great expert on sexual unhappiness had to believe that civilization outweighed its discontents: the alternative – that we'd made ourselves miserable for nothing – was too terrible to contemplate.

Did humans ever live in sexual freedom? Was work ever fun? Did we always privilege our immediate genetic offspring over other members of the community? The debate continues in our time. Christopher Ryan and Cacilda Jethá, in their study "Sex at Dawn," side with Engels, citing anthropological data about numerous hunter-gatherer societies that aren't monogamous, don't have nuclear families, and don't valorize paternal certainty. They argue that this was the norm before the Neolithic revolution, that promiscuity had once fostered cooperation and reduced violence among our tribal ancestors, and that a false belief in the "naturalness" of monogamy is responsible for myriad social ills: nineteenth-century foundling hospitals, the stoning of women in Iran, the destruction of numerous American political careers. Such views bring them into conflict with Steven Pinker, whose recent book "The Better Angels of Our Nature" argues that society is at a current all-time high in peacefulness, and that the hunter-gatherers were massacring and barbecuing each other for hundreds of millennia before the cultivation of wheat.

Schmidt's view is closer to Pinker's. "They were trained killers, nothing else," he says of the hunter-gatherers. He believes that Göbekli Tepe was built by a laboring class, maybe even by slaves. In his view, the reason that agriculture stuck, even though it meant more work and worse food, was that an élite caste had a vested interest in the new system: "Ninety per cent had to work, and ten per cent lived by wealth. The élite wanted to keep their advantage, and they had the power to do it." If Schmidt is right and a form of social exploitation was already observable before farming, then agriculture wasn't a disaster, or any kind of game changer: the human condition was, as Freud implies, always at least as bad as it is now.

"Was there any time when it wasn't like that?" I asked. "Like, a hundred thousand years ago?"

Schmidt shrugged. "Humans don't change so much," he said. "The background of our knowledge is getting bigger. But our daily behavior is the same. We are all *Homo sapiens*."

I asked Schmidt what he thought of the allegorical reading of the Fall of Man as the shift to agriculture. He objected that the Garden of Eden was a garden, and thus represented a horticultural rather than a hunter-gatherer mode of subsistence. Schmidt's resistance to metaphors and speculation is, in a way, part of the job. "You're a scientist, you're professional," he told me. "What we're looking at – it's material culture. We aren't imagining things we can't see." Imagination is always projection: to guess how Neolithic people might have felt about anything was to assume, doubtless incorrectly, that they felt the way we would have felt about it. And yet, with no imagination at all, it's difficult to see how any interpretation is possible. As Jens Notroff put it, "Without any imagination, this is all a pile of rubbish."

After my last afternoon at Göbekli Tepe, I decided to devote the rest of the day to the other Urfa pilgrimage – the Abraham one. I walked along teeming sidewalks, among street venders selling pomegranates, lottery tickets, novelty Korans, fresh pistachio nuts, sherbet, bitter coffee, photocopies. One man was literally selling snake oil – a thing I had never seen before – in addition to ant-egg oil, hair tonic, and unscented soap for pilgrims. Handbills advertised a conference called "Understanding the Prophet Abraham in the 21st Century." A psychiatrist with a storefront office specialized in "ailments of the nerves and soul." Most restaurants had signs that said "WE HAVE A FAMILY ROOM!" – meaning that the main dining room was for men only. About eighty-five per cent of the pedestrians were men. Nearly all the women were wearing head scarves, or even burkas. I saw one woman so pious that her burka didn't even have an opening for her eyes. She was leaving a cell-phone store, accompanied by a teen-age boy wearing a T-shirt that said "RELAX, MAN," over a picture of an ice-cream cone playing an electric guitar. You wouldn't think an ice-cream cone *could* play an electric guitar, or would want to. I was reminded of Schmidt's hypothesis that hybrid creatures and monsters, unknown to Neolithic man, are particular to highly developed cultures – cultures which have achieved distance from and fear of nature. If archeologists of the future found this T-shirt, they would know ours had been a civilization of great refinement.

I reached a large park with manicured lawns, a rose garden, gushing fountains, and shady tea gardens, and made my way to a rectangular stone-lined pool crammed with fat gray carp, indicating the spot where Nimrod failed to burn up Abraham. It's said that anyone who eats one of these carp will go blind. All kinds of people – tough-looking men in black leather jackets, women in shapeless trenchcoats and head scarves, two girls dressed like Arabian princesses with gold coins on their foreheads – were buying fish food from venders and hurling it into the pond by the fistful. The sacred carp accumulated in a great heap below the surface of the water, their gaping circular mouths angled upward.

The cave where Abraham might have been born had been divided into two caves: one for men, one for women. I went into the women's entrance hall, where a low-ceilinged stone tunnel led to the holy site. A giant, headless lump of cloth appeared in the mouth of the tunnel, and came shuffling toward me. This turned out to be a woman exiting the cave backward. When the passage was clear again, I stooped double and made my way inside.

Greenish-yellow light shimmered on the rough stone walls. Behind a large glass window, like an aquarium display, a spring was burbling in a rocky cave interior. Women were gathered around a motion-activated faucet that dispensed water from the holy spring. They waved their hands under the tap, like people in an airport bathroom. Nobody could predict what motion would turn on the holy water. Having taken my turn at the faucet, I proceeded to the prayer area and knelt on the silk carpet, behind an extremely thin young woman in a black dress and head scarf. Palms upturned, she swayed back and forth for a minute or two, then suddenly flung her body forward and touched her forehead to the carpet. Several times, the young woman repeated this motion of tremendous beauty and fierceness. I thought about the power of the sacred: originating, if the archeologists are to be believed, in the most material expediencies of the body – how and what to eat – it overtakes the soul, making Neolithic man build Göbekli Tepe and making him bury it, sweeping through the millennia, generating monuments, strivings, vast inner landscapes. I thought about history, and the riddle of the Sphinx: what goes on four legs in the morning, on two legs at noon, and on three legs in the evening? Some people say that history is progress: isn't this just a reflection of how we're born, tiny, weak, and speechless, and then go on to build cathedrals and fly to the moon? When others say that history is a decline from a golden age, isn't this because youth is so brief and we regret it for so long?

I thought about Abraham – Father of Multitudes, builder of monotheism – and about the covenant, when Abraham was unhappy because he had no children and was going to have to leave his property to a servant, and God promised him as many offspring as there are stars in the sky. This covenant fulfilled the two great demands of the agricultural order: land and paternally certain offspring. If Göbekli Tepe was the Garden of Eden, where these demands first came into being, then there is a certain logic in the identification of Urfa with Abraham's birthplace. Viewed in this light, as one big story, it may seem as if the last generation at Göbekli Tepe, when they buried their temple and embarked on a new way of life, didn't, after all, succeed in severing their ties to the future.

An Archaeology of Sustenance:
The Endangered Market Gardens of Istanbul

CHANTEL WHITE, ALEKSANDAR SHOPOV
AND MARTA OSTOVICH

Gardeners take a break in Crazy Toma's *bostan* in Istanbul; the second person from the right is eating a leaf of delicious Yedikule lettuce. (Photo by Rıza Bey, by permission.)

It looks easy, but it isn't. In the late afternoon sunshine, master gardener Mehmet Bey deftly maneuvers a wooden rake to prepare *maşula*, rectangular beds of soil with raised edges that give the garden a chessboard-like appearance. A colorful variety of vegetables including purslane, peppers, lettuce, and dill flourish here. Within the *maşula*, these vegetables receive a perfect amount of sunlight. The edges protect the plants from the surface wind and hold in moisture during the final weeks of summer. Mehmet Bey, eyes toward the soil, works swiftly across the garden terrace, each action parsed down to essential movements.

A visit to Mehmet Bey's garden is like stepping out of Istanbul, even though it is located at the heart of the city, in the neighborhood of Yedikule. Large-leafed fig trees shield much of the direct summer sunlight, and it is a full 10 degrees cooler here than on the city sidewalks. Gardeners are busy with their quiet daily work, loading produce into market baskets and slicing large red tomatoes for drying. The sensory experience of the gardens is powerful: fresh, fragrant leaves of mint and dill, bright red radishes and deep purple basil, sticky figs, and tart cherries. Sitting in the cool shade beneath a network of hanging trombetta squash, one begins to feel a different sense of the passage of time. To paraphrase the author Ken Kesey, in the gardens one can begin to feel time overlap itself.

Up until the mid-20th century, there were hundreds of market gardens in Istanbul. One garden could produce dozens of tons of produce and their average size was around 10,000 m². Today, the Yedikule gardens are the only historic market-garden complex that remains in Istanbul. Each element of these gardens has its own history, which intertwines with that of the city. The topsoil, for example, is the product of both natural processes and gardening activities. Full of living microbes, it is also filled with ancient Byzantine pottery sherds and discarded city refuse from past centuries. The crops each tell individual stories of domestication from across the globe, and many have been cultivated in Istanbul's gardens for at least 1,000 years.

Known in Turkish as *bostans*, the gardens are a meeting place for old and new crops, and they exist within a complex cycle of planting, growth, and harvest. They are spaces where traditional agricultural methods such as the *maşula* are often applied to new cultivars, where new local residents often reside, and are a location of shifting economic concerns. These gardens have sustained city residents through periods of food scarcity and even famine. During an eight-year siege by the Ottoman Sultan Bayezid I at the end of the 14th century, residents were able to survive the winter months by relying almost entirely upon vegetables – cabbage, turnips, and beetroot – produced in such gardens within the city.

Today, the urban gardens of Istanbul are under extraordinary pressure.

There are few safety measures in place to protect them from rampant development. Since the Yedikule gardens were partially destroyed in the 1960s, they have been subject to other episodes of destruction, most recently in 1999, 2004, and the summer of 2013. The current multi-million-dollar development project, whose first phase began and was partially carried out in July of 2013, may result in the complete obliteration of the remaining gardens and the wholesale displacement of gardening families.

Nowhere is the overlapping of time more apparent than in the physical location of the gardens in the neighborhood of Yedikule. The military fortification walls of Constantinople, first constructed in the fifth century A.D., are home to an extensive network of urban *bostans*. The ancient stones of the walls glow at sunset, as leafy green vegetables planted between the arched double-walls – a space where there was once a moat – soak up the last light. Nearby is the Seven Towers Fortress, or Yedikule, which gave both the neighborhood and the gardens their name. Built immediately after the conquest of Constantinople in 1453 and directly adjacent to the gardens, its star shape exemplified new fortification designs adapting to the rise of gunpowder. It also heralded the rise of a new neighborhood and a new garden complex.

Since 1985, Istanbul's fortification walls and their immediate surroundings have been recognized as part of the Historic Areas of Istanbul UNESCO World Heritage Site. The walls offer a rare example of Byzantine military architecture dating back to the reign of emperor Theodosius II (A.D. 408–450). Ruling over a growing urban center, Theodosius expanded the city's limits along its western perimeter. The new fortification included a wide moat, two massive walls, and towers. To a traveler approaching the city from the west, these fortifications sprawled across the horizon would have presented an awe-inspiring sight.

Yet despite their historical significance, the city walls have never existed in isolation. Rather, since their construction, the walls have been integral to a network of trade, exchange, and agricultural productivity. This is attested by numerous historical documents and maps from the Byzantine and Ottoman periods. An edict in the Theodosian Code, for example, written just after the walls were built, records that the emperor compensated residents for agricultural land that had been lost to wall construction. And while the upper floors of the fortification towers were reserved for military use, this edict offers the ground floor for landowners' private use, presumably for storing things like farm equipment.

In the succeeding centuries of Byzantine and Ottoman rule, agriculture and gardening continued around the Theodosian walls in ways that were constantly in transformation. This history is still visible today around Yedikule. Extant archaeological features speak to the large-scale agrarian transformation of the landscape in the 16th through 19th centuries. One example is the circular stone waterwells (*kuyular*) built during this period that can still be seen throughout the Yedikule neighborhood and gardens. Despite their large size – as much as 5 m in diameter and 20 m deep – these Ottoman wells lie hidden in the gardens among stands of fig trees. It is only by pushing away branches and peering down into the shadows that one can actually see their magnitude and depth. One can almost think of the waterwells as towers in reverse, stretching down into the darkness and every bit as unnerving as the Seven Towers Fortress nearby. Most of the surviving gardens along the walls still use a well as their primary means of irrigation, albeit with electric pumps instead of the waterwheels that were powered by horses until about a century ago.

One of the earliest historical records of a waterwell near Yedikule is found in an Ottoman survey of the city of Istanbul from 1455, two years after the Ottoman conquest of Constantinople. The same document notes the presence of an orchard tended by a resident named Kir Liko, located just north of Yedikule near the Silivrikapı city gate. By the 17th century, legal documents mentioning the Yedikule gardens and their associated features became much more commonplace. Many deeds from this period, endowed by high-ranking bureaucrats, mention these *bostans* and their waterwells as part of the endowed properties of schools and mosques. In the mid-17th century, a grand vizier even endowed land in Yedikule featuring a *kuyu*. Known as Bayram Paşa, the wealthy vizier used the income from the gardens to fund a school and a dervish lodge that he constructed in the city. Two gardens in Yedikule, just within the city walls, bear his name in an early 18th-century survey, which also records almost 1,400 gardeners that worked in the city proper.

Despite the presence of the waterwells, irrigating vegetables and fruits in Yedikule was a more difficult task in comparison with other parts of the city. The neighborhood is situated on the seventh hill of Istanbul and accessing water from this elevation is challenging. In contrast to older garden complexes such as the well-known Langa gardens in the Lykos valley, which were close to a large stream, the waterwells in Yedikule needed to be deeper. One water source was a natural stream that used to flow just outside the Theodosian walls, at the bottom of the seventh hill. However, in the 1950s the stream was piped, buried, and paved over by a four-lane highway. Walking along the walls today, you can still imagine the stream gurgling through underground channels and ducts, and racing out to sea – inaccessible to the gardens just a few meters above.

Photographs from the early 20th century indicate that the chessboard pattern of planting beds (*maşula*), irrigated by the wells, have been an essential feature of the gardens for nearly a century or longer. When water is pumped from a well, it is stored in a cistern that is elevated slightly above it and strategically positioned so that every part of the garden can be irrigated using the force of gravity, flowing down into radiating channels that hydrate each of the planting beds. Larger plots for growing lettuce, tomatoes, and peppers are bisected by long irrigation channels, while the rectangular *maşula* plots, measuring about 1 by 1.5 m, are individually opened for irrigation: the gardener, moving from *maşula* to *maşula* in the direction of the flowing water, uses a hoe to divert water from the irrigation canal into each of the planting beds. The surfaces of *maşula* are created meticulously to be as level as possible, so that when waters enters, it is equally distributed and each of the plants receives the same amount of water. The borders of the *maşula*, around ten cm high, prevent surface winds from taking away precious moisture during the hot summer months.

When it's irrigation time, everyone leaves the terraces and planting beds except for the gardeners. "Get out of the *maşula!*" a gardener called to us one afternoon. "I'm going to irrigate!" We left quickly, as though a dam had broken and water might have swept us away. Watering the gardens, however, is a carefully controlled operation. In their organizational pattern, the *maşulas* not only save water, but also enable different varieties of plants to be grown separately, yet side-by-side. They can also be used to designate spaces in the garden for the cultivation and collection of new seeds. From above, the gardeners resemble chess players, moving within a series of carefully tended squares.

Today's gardeners in Yedikule are primarily Turkish immigrants or descendants of immigrants from the coastal region of Kastamonu on the southern shore of the Black Sea. Their techniques of cultivation have been acquired from previous generations of gardeners already living in Istanbul, mostly families from Ottoman Macedonia and Albania whose ancestors arrived in the city at the end of the 19th century. By and large, the vegetable gardens of Istanbul have always been operated by immigrants. An Ottoman survey of gardeners from 1734 suggests that this pattern was already in place by then. Of the 1,381 gardeners working in 344 *bostans* within the city walls, most came from villages near western Macedonian cities such as Manastir (Bitola), Vodena (Edessa), Selanik, and Ohrid, and a smaller number from Albania. Their personal names provide further evidence of their origins – Petre, Riste, Hristo, Grozdan – and suggest that the gardeners of 18th-century Istanbul were primarily a Slavic-speaking population.

The influx of so many immigrants into the city (during what was a socially and economically unstable period in the Western Balkans) had a profound impact on Istanbul. On the one hand, the increase in available labor set the stage for a major increase in agricultural production in the city during the late 17th and 18th centuries, while at the same decreasing the costs for construction projects such as waterwells. On the other, as Istanbul was settled by migrants from both the Balkans and Anatolia, the population increase and shift also came with a change in the demand for food. Fruits and vegetables produced in the city now found a ready market.

The descendants of these older waves of gardeners in Yedikule were affected by a major social upheaval that occurred in the 1950s, in which many orthodox Christian families were compelled to leave the city, taking with them generations of knowledge about local crops and garden histories. One such casualty was Crazy Toma's Lettuce Garden, a social hub for gardeners in Yedikule.

Crazy Toma's Lettuce Garden no longer exists, but it is remembered by some of the gardeners who once spent long afternoons relaxing there in the 1950s. One such gardener is Rıza Bey, a sharply dressed man in his mid-70s whose family owned a garden in Yedikule until 1963, when they were forced to sell their land for a housing project. When we met Rıza Bey in a local restaurant this past summer, he was quick to show us a few worn black-and-white photographs of the gardens, including one of Crazy Toma's Lettuce Garden. In this photo, a young Rıza Bey and his friends sat smiling around a small table in a garden cafe. "He was *Rum* (that is to say, Greek Orthodox), and he was Turkish," Rıza says, pointing to different friends in the photo. "And he was Greek Orthodox too. It didn't matter; we all got along." In the end, however, it did matter, and the days of Crazy Toma's Lettuce Garden ended with the government-organized Istanbul Pogrom of 1955, which transformed entire neighborhoods in the city, including Yedikule. Greek Orthodox churches were destroyed, and many Christian homes and business were burned to the ground.

After the Pogrom, it was easier for the municipality to expropriate agricultural land and other property for large development projects, including the highway along the Theodosian walls and the Vatan boulevard over the ancient Lykos, or Bayram Paşa stream. Many Greek Orthodox gardeners, including Crazy Toma and his sons, abandoned the neighborhood soon after. The famous taverns of Yedikule, most of which were operated by Greek Orthodox residents, were shut down and thus no longer needed produce from the gardens. The local economy was left in shambles. Nearly all the gardens in the neighborhood changed hands, and an influx of immigrants from the Black Sea in the 1960s began the most recent urban gardening wave.

Crazy Toma's Lettuce Garden is now a mosque complex located next to the Seven Towers Fortress. We visited the overgrown garden of the mosque with Rıza Bey and held up his old photograph, trying to identify the exact position from which it was taken. The old garden seemed to come alive again for him as he remembered his fellow gardeners. Then he quietly remarked that after the Pogrom "these gardens were never the same." One important loss was the unique type of lettuce that made them famous across the city. It was known as Yedikule lettuce (*marul*), and the gardeners of Yedikule were experts in growing the largest and best-tasting lettuce in the region. Yedikule lettuce was so special, in fact, that it was the only thing on the menu at Crazy Toma's Lettuce Garden cafe, whose patrons flocked from all over the city.

But how could Crazy Toma's garden cafe *only* serve lettuce? we asked dubiously. Who eats lettuce for fun? But the large-leafed cos lettuce from this neighborhood was renowned for its taste, size, and juiciness, or even buttery flavor. Its young leaves were eaten fresh with only a little added salt. Closer examination of Rıza Bey's photograph confirmed that his friends were sitting with a large metal pan filled with lettuce leaves. One man can be seen holding up a young lettuce leaf, smiling and preparing to eat it as soon as the photo was taken.

By the 1980s, Yedikule lettuce had completely disappeared from Yedikule. Lettuce requires ample space to grow, and too much space had already been lost by this point due to rezoning and real estate speculation. To lose this unique lettuce cultivar was a damaging blow to the botanical history of the city, but one could argue that it was only one lettuce variety, grown within one neighborhood. Yet the same thing has happened across the city. In the neighborhood of Arnavutköy, once famous for its fragrant pink strawberries, rampant housing construction has destroyed all the historical strawberry gardens in the area. In Çengelköy, on the Asian side of the Bosphorus, extensive gardens once home to a small, tasty variety of cucumber – a well-known local delicacy – have been paved over with concrete. The same is true for the gardens at Langa, the source of a long, thin cucumber variety, replaced first by a desolate industrial area and, more recently, by the new Yenikapı subway station.

Each of these local crops has a fascinating back-story. According to the *Geoponika*, a Byzantine agricultural manual from the 10th century, the planting schedule for Istanbul's gardens included a number of vegetables such as lettuce, cabbage, beets, carrots, onions, and turnips. In more recent centuries, new crops have made their way into the gardens through the diffusion of American produce, Mediterranean foodways, and new agricultural practices. Potatoes and tomatoes have become integral ingredients in Turkish cuisine over the past hundred years, even while maintaining traces of their South American origins through their common Turkish names, *patates* and *domates.*

Other crops mentioned in the *Geoponika* are now often found as weeds in the modern gardens, including mallow and orach. A botanical palimpsest endures: new crops such as Thai basil grow tall, while ancient crops quietly persist along the margins.

Cultivars, or unique crop varieties, are developed over time, based on two important factors. The first is human intervention – the intentional selection and propagation of plants with desirable, inheritable traits (taste, crunch, smell). Yet this does not completely explain why lettuce grew so well in Yedikule, or why cucumbers flourished in Çengelköy. Rather, the answer also lies in the specific microclimates of Istanbul's urban gardens. The city exists within a transitional climatic zone, so that its gardens experience variations of Mediterranean, Oceanic, and Continental climates, depending upon their locations. Hotter, drier Mediterranean conditions are found along the southern edge of the peninsula (Yedikule, Langa), while cooler, rainier Oceanic conditions exist farther north (Sarıyer, Arnavutköy). There are also substantial differences in soil type, temperature, sunlight, and aspect. Each garden in Istanbul has its individual *terroir* of sorts, a unique set of environmental characteristics that benefit certain crop species. The Yedikule gardens, with their southern aspect and abundant sunshine during the summer months, were particularly suited for large-leafed cos lettuce, which originated on the sunny Greek island of Kos.

When a neighborhood garden was destroyed, so too was its *terroir*. For some cultivars, seeds were preserved and are now grown in other parts of Turkey. One can buy "Yedikule lettuce" and "Çengelköy cucumbers" at the market, but these vegetables are not grown anywhere near Yedikule or Çengelköy today, nor do they taste the same. The place-name has stuck as a brand-name of sorts, calling to mind the juicy lettuce that Yedikule gardeners once produced, or the crunchy little cucumbers of Çengelköy. But older residents of the city know the difference. They remember the intense fragrance of Arnavutköy strawberries, so strong that you could smell strawberries all the way across the Bosphorus when they ripened in the summer. They remember the delicious taste of the Kavak fig from *bostans* in the north of the city, with skin so thin that the entire fruit could be eaten without peeling, a fruit that has all but disappeared from Istanbul's markets.

Today most fruits and vegetables are grown far from Istanbul and are then trucked in to urban markets. Whether it is lettuce, cucumbers, artichokes, strawberries, or figs, one common characteristic of the historic Istanbul cultivars is that they had to be eaten fresh. These are not crops that travel well, nor can they be stored for long periods of time. The benefit of Istanbul's *bostan* system was the immediate accessibility of fresh produce, and local cultivar types reflect this abbreviated window of garden-to-market freshness. Without the city's gardens and their unique *terroir*, historical varieties of vegetables and fruits are now dying out.

The Istanbul branch of the Association of Archaeologists submitted a letter to the Istanbul Archaeology Museums in 2013 detailing the destruction of both the Yedikule gardens and ancient walls wrought by bulldozers. In 2014 a report was presented by archaeologists to the UNESCO World Heritage Centre concerning the need to protect the gardens. To be clear, the area of Yedikule that remains protected, at least on paper, includes not only the Theodosian walls – the outer and inner walls, associated terraces, and moat – but also the areas on either side of the walls, which includes the gardens. Despite this protection, both the walls and the gardens have been irreparably damaged. In 2006, bulldozers removed a sizeable section of the walls near Yedikule fortress. A gated community, Yedikule Konaklar, was built in 2010, directly over the site of a former *bostan*. The community sits facing the gaping hole in the Theodosian walls, which is still visible today.

In the summer of 2013, three further *bostans* were partially or completely destroyed to make way for housing, restaurants, and – ironically – a "green space" (a park). The local gardeners, who were given only a few days' warning before bulldozers showed up in their fields in the middle of the night, rushed to harvest their crops as bulldozers plowed under all remaining plants. The Theodosian wall abutting these gardens was scraped with backhoes to remove over a meter of soil from its surface, most likely undermining its structural integrity in the process. Rubble fill was then dumped on top of the healthy topsoil in order to level out the ground surface. The gardens were buried alive.

That summer some Istanbul residents and scholars joined the gardeners in defending the *bostans*, in an unprecedented expression of solidarity. Roles mingled: the gardeners gave lectures to their supporters on the history of the Yedikule gardens, and their supporters, many of whom had just discovered the long history of farming in the city, pitched in and got their hands dirty. Mehmet and his colleagues instructed young *Istanbuliots* on how to hoe *maşula* in an attempt to show the public and the Municipality that the loss was not only soil but also living knowledge. Gardeners working in the undestroyed *bostans* welcomed evicted gardeners and activists and organized a campaign for reclaiming the destroyed gardens. From the ruins of the *bostans* a new struggle ensued.

One year later, we returned to the destroyed garden area in Yedikule and discovered a resurgence of plant life. Weeds had colonized the fields over the winter, many of which were immediately recognizable: mallow, orach, *vlita*, mint. Some of the earliest cultivated plants in the Istanbul gardens had reappeared, the same crops mentioned in the *Geoponika* farming manual over 1,000 years ago where they are described as food. Tenacious weeds, yet still just as edible as they were during the 10th century, these plants provide enduring evidence of the agricultural legacy of the *bostans*.

The Yedikule gardens are a living history. They contain plants that are alive – varieties found nowhere else – within a set of unique ecosystems. They are also a way of life that comprises not only the plants, the environment, the city walls, and other archaeological features, but also the day-to-day interactions between the gardeners, their labor and their struggle. Heritage is much more than the sum of these cultural and natural elements: it is also intangible, as recognized by UNESCO's 2003 *Convention for Safeguarding of Intangible Cultural Heritage*. What is intangible in the Yedikule garden complex is the knowledge that each gardener possesses about specific crops and the techniques of cultivating them – knowledge localized for each *bostan* and its growing conditions. Some of this information can be communicated orally, but most gardening activities need to be learned by doing. Learning how to create the perfect *maşula* planting beds from gardener Mehmet Bey is next to impossible without a rake in your hands. Bodily experience is essential to all agricultural knowledge, and it is an intangible form of cultural heritage.

Gardening actions are, as archaeologist Alessandra Ricci argues, an expression of social practices passed down through generations. Even as gardening methods change over time, they reflect the creativity of individual gardeners and the changing tastes of the city's residents. The history of the gardens provides a window into the labor practices of immigrant populations whose vital role in feeding the city has been overlooked.

The future of the Yedikule gardens hangs in the balance. While the Metropolitan Municipality of Istanbul included the gardens along the walls in a set of plans drafted in 2011 to protect various cultural sites in the Old City, they have yet to implement or enforce any protections – and, in fact, it was the Metropolitan Municipality itself that carried out the most recent destruction in 2013. In the meantime, gardeners such as Mehmet Bey not only continue the cycle of irrigating, planting, weeding, and harvesting, but have also become engaged in a struggle against neoliberal urban development. Left unchecked, these politics will bury the last living traces of the Istanbul *bostans*, and with them, 1,600 years of agricultural history.

> *This talk is like stamping new coins. They pile up,*
> *while the real work is being done outside*
> *by someone digging in the ground.*
> Rumi

The Quest:
Who Were the First Americans?

Chip Colwell

George McJunkin, the black cowboy and amateur archaeologist who discovered the Folsom kill site in 1908. (Photo from Denver Museum of Nature and Science Archives [0085-719].)

It is a strange fact that the fate of American archaeology should be tied so closely to a thunderous cloudburst that happened to have settled over the headwaters of the Dry Cimarron River one late evening in 1908. As the rain cascaded through the valley in torrents, golden pyramids of hay, harvested from surrounding farms days before, were washed downriver, piling up along with downed trees and other debris at a railroad bridge west of Folsom, New Mexico. As the dark storm lingered, this temporary dam burst, sending a 20-foot wall of water surging towards the small, helpless town. By morning, the survivors counted 17 dead. Most of Folsom was swept away, as though it had never existed at all.

Several weeks later, George McJunkin, the foreman at Crowfoot Ranch, was checking the damage done to the fences by the flood. He was not your average cowboy. Born a slave in Texas in 1856, McJunkin later worked as a wrangler driving cattle from Texas to Kansas. He survived blizzards, stampedes, and Indian attacks, and eventually made his way to Folsom. He befriended a family there, who taught him to read and encouraged his interest in natural history; he started collecting exotica, like fossils, minerals, and arrowheads – even an Indian skull. That day McJunkin followed one stretch of fencing until it fell tangled into a newly incised arroyo, cut down 10 vertical feet. As he peered into the fissure, his eyes focused on what appeared to be a large object, pearly white, protruding from the base of the arroyo. Curious, he dismounted from his horse and slid down the ravine. On his knees, he pulled out wire clippers and excavated several massive bones from the mud. A wide smile broke across his face: the flood had exposed a deeply buried site. McJunkin had probably read enough about archaeology to understand that the animals here had died a long time ago.

In the years that followed he told everyone about his "bone pit," although few paid him any attention. One man he told was Carl Schwachheim, an amateur collector who lived in nearby Raton. But it was not until 1922, the year McJunkin died, that Schwachheim visited the site with a friend, a banker named Fred Howarth. In 1926, the two succeeded in getting the attention of scholars when they traveled to Denver and met with Jesse D. Figgins, the director of the Colorado Museum of Natural History. Predictably, perhaps, for decades only a few minor publications would give passing credit to a nameless "Negro cowboy."

By this time, Figgins and a fellow paleontologist at the museum, Harold Cook, hoped to resolve a critical dispute. When did Native Americans first arrive in North America? Many believed that they had come when the continent was covered by glaciers and full of mammoths, giant sloths, lions, llamas, musk oxen, horses, and bison. But no one knew for certain. This single question had become one of the most important for late 19th-

and early 20th-century archaeology, because its answer meant that Native American cultures had witnessed either a long unfolding (and so could make a deep claim to the continent's ancient past), or a much more recent arrival (and so merely superficial claims, as newcomers themselves). Resolution of this issue had also become one of the most vexing problems, on account of the real difficulty of finding early sites – and definitive evidence of dates associated with them – in the vastness of the American continent.

In the early 1920s, the Colorado Museum staff had come across several tantalizing sites, but they, like everyone else, had still not found the smoking arrowhead. When Harold Cook was presented with the bones from Folsom in 1926, he thought that they might be from an extinct species of bison – meaning that the site was perhaps very old. Quickly, plans were laid to excavate. Several months later, the crew uncovered a spear point, definitive evidence of a human presence at the site. But they were unlucky enough to find it in loose soil, rather than securely in context with the extinct bison bones. Perhaps the spear point came from a different stratigraphic layer, or a different time period? Notable archaeologists swiftly dismissed the find.

The next summer, soon after excavations resumed, Schwachheim contacted Figgins. "I found an arrow or spear point at noon," he wrote. "Thought perhaps some of your doubters would like to see the evidence in the matrix and in place." Figgins dispatched telegrams inviting the country's scientists to New Mexico and instructed Schwachheim to guard the find "every minute." Three of America's most pre-eminent archaeologists soon arrived. They scrutinized the discovery and unanimously agreed. The spear point – later to be described as a unique type called the Folsom Point – lodged between the two rib bones of the extinct bison was decisive proof, given the estimated age of the extinct bison, that Native Americans had arrived in Ice Age America, more than 10,000 years ago.

Who are Native Americans? For more than 500 years, this question has ebbed and flowed in the minds of philosophers, theologians, historians, and conquerors – the answer stubbornly elusive. It is a thrilling question, because even today there is not yet a full sense of the answer. These are mostly what Donald Rumsfeld would call "known unknowns." Nearly all agree there were waves of migrations from Asia, with the first people traveling across Beringia, the land-bridge that once spanned Siberia and Alaska. But when? More than 20,000 years – some 1,600 human generations – separates these scholars' estimates of when Native Americans first arrived on the continent. There are others who hypothesize a prehistoric migration from Europe. Native Americans' own origin myths, meanwhile, emphasize that they were born here, from the earth itself, in time immemorial. For nearly a century, the origin of Native Americans has been one of the hottest questions in archaeology, and in just the last few years a string of discoveries has kept the field in tumult. These are concrete questions of time and place, but their answers provoke existential debate about identity and belonging. The crux: who, if anyone, can claim the first Americans as their kin?

Christopher Columbus made landfall in the Bahamas on October 12, 1492, where, as he wrote, he was met by naked "natives of the land." Columbus named them *indios*, believing he had arrived at the Indian subcontinent's outer edge. Only 14 years later, another conquistador, Vasco Nuñez de Balboa, crossed the Isthmus of Panama. Arriving at the Pacific, Balboa understood, in a single moment, that an ocean separated Asia from America: this New World was not part of the Old World at all. The origins of *los indios* abruptly became a profound mystery.

The debate about America's Indians consumed Europe's courts, churches, and universities. A few were doubtful that they were humans at all, but most looked to their own cultural touchstones for evidence. Were they among Noah's eight survivors? Were they the progeny of Atlantis, the legendary civilization beyond the western sea? For centuries most guessed that American Indians were lost Greeks, Phoenicians, Egyptians, Tartars, Carthaginians, Welshmen, Norsemen, Celts, or Israelites.

These guesses were finally annulled in the aftermath of the Enlightenment. The estimate of Bishop Ussher that the universe was created on Sunday, 23 October 4,004 B.C. was undermined by Isaac Newton's calculations of the earth's age, Georges Cuvier's analyses of extinctions through the fossil record, and Charles Darwin's theory of evolution by means of natural selection, which provided a framework for biological change over the eons, along with numerous other discoveries great and small. By the 1860s, the presence of ancient stone tools, as well as Neanderthals (an extinct species of *Homo* living about 40,000–200,000 years ago) in Europe affirmed the existence of an ancient period of early human development; it was labeled the Paleolithic, from Greek *palaios* (old) and *lithos* (stone).

But was there an equivalent American Stone Age? When they began to look around, amateur collectors found simple stone artifacts in glacial deposits (and thus, by definition, *palaios*). For a moment, the budding discipline agreed that the continent's human history was ancient. But then a critique emerged from the powerful Smithsonian Institution. The archaeologist William Henry Holmes argued that "primitive"-looking artifacts were not necessarily old, while the so-called "father" of physical anthropology, Aleš Hrdlička, reasoned that, since Neanderthal fossils couldn't be found in the Americas, the New World could not have had a Paleolithic period. These were the pro- and anti-Paleolithic factions that had been locked in a stalemate three decades long, when one summer day a trowel hit a spear point made of translucent brown stone lodged between two ribs of an extinct bison outside Folsom, New Mexico.

With time, a consensus emerged that migrants traversed Beringia into the Americas about 13,500 years ago. These first Americans came to be known as Clovis (named after another site in New Mexico), which by 12,500 years ago developed into the Folsom tradition. Although Folsom was shown not to be the oldest archaeological type-site in the Americas, it continued to be celebrated for first demonstrating that humans lived in the American Ice Age. For half a century, Folsom, it seemed, had settled the debate. But then, as often happens in science, it turned out that the debate wasn't settled at all. A few began to ask: When precisely did the first people arrive in the Americas? Where exactly did they come from? And what did Native Americans have to say about their own origins?

Eight years ago I took a new job as a curator at the Denver Museum of Nature and Science – the same museum, but with a new name, that had sponsored the discovery of the Folsom point in 1927. Down the hall from me was my colleague, Steve Holen, an avuncular white-haired archaeologist, who, by both his position and disposition, had inherited Jesse Figgins' contentious search for the earliest human sites in North America. I had heard Steve's work would upend everything I thought I knew about who the first Native Americans were.

I soon stopped by Steve's office. He stood by a table scattered with ivory-hued bones he had excavated from the New Nebraska Mammoth Site. Quiet and unassuming, his eyes suddenly sparkled when he handed me a fragment of a mammoth thigh bone, as dense as a nugget of gold. Beneath a veneer of calm scientific rationality, Steve's excitement brimmed. He pointed out how the bone tool was like its counterparts in stone. The bone fragment was broken off from a larger piece (a "core") and then refined into a cutting tool – an Ice Age paring knife. It seemed obvious to me the bone tool must have been made by human hands. Then, like a magician, Steve offered the reveal: the New Nebraska Mammoth Site dates to 33,000 years ago.

David J. Meltzer, one of today's foremost archaeologists, wrote in his 2009 book *First Peoples in a New World: Colonizing Ice Age America* that the possibilities for documenting a pre-Clovis migration – sites that date before 13,500 years ago – have waned over the years. In 1964, one list identified 50 possible pre-Clovis sites; in 1976, the list was winnowed down to 35; by 1988, the list had evaporated to five. As Meltzer explains, the list has continually narrowed, because for a site to have convincing pre-Clovis evidence it must meet three key criteria: (1) unambiguous dates derived from scientific methods, (2) clear evidence of a human presence, and (3) a well documented, undisturbed geological context. Easy – except that it's not.

Even the most promising sites are overcast by suspicion. Meadowcroft, a rockshelter in Pennsylvania, has produced dates of 14,250 years ago, but some critics think the samples used for the dates were contaminated (problem: criterion 1). Another contender, also a rockshelter, is Pedra Furada in Brazil, where the oldest dates reach back an astounding 50,000 years – quadrupling the possible depth of human antiquity in the Americas. On closer inspection, however, many have doubted whether the 600 quartz cobbles from the lowest levels, broken into what were claimed to be tools, were really tools at all (problem: criterion 2). The most compelling site is Monte Verde, in southern Chile. Excavated between 1977 and 1985, Monte Verde has an unambiguous human presence, with well-preserved huts, hearths, plants, shellfish, eggshells, and mastodon remains. In one of the lowest levels of the site, the dates average 12,500 years ago, with the oldest date at 13,565 (plus or minus 250) years ago – just a little older than any Clovis site, but suggestive of a much earlier initial migration into the Americas, given the site's great distance from Siberia. Still, a handful of archaeologists remain unconvinced. They point to discrepancies in how some of the key artifacts were mapped and recorded (problem: criterion 3).

Steve Holen himself has doubts about these sites. But he has even stronger doubts about whether Clovis represents the first Native Americans. "I don't accept things as dogma. I always questioned arguments from authority. So I questioned the Clovis model since my first years in college," Steve recently told me. "When I first started doing excavations, they'd say 'Don't go into those older deposits!' But I was always looking into them."

Steve's search for the first Americans was a long time coming. He grew up on a Nebraska farm full of ancient Indian sites. Relatives living nearby ran a gravel pit. To their consternation, mammoth bones often clogged the machinery. But Steve was seduced. "By 11 years old I was more interested in collecting Indian artifacts than farming," he said. When he entered college at the University of Nebraska, it seemed inevitable that Steve would study the first Native Americans who lived alongside the great mammoth.

In 2013, Steve published a book chapter with his wife, Kathy (also an archaeologist), summarizing a decade of work. They nonchalantly write – as if offering a grocery list instead of re-writing American archaeology – that across the Great Plains there are seven pre-Clovis sites that date between 14,000 and 20,000 years ago. Then they up the ante and list seven more sites dating between 20,000 and 40,000 years ago. Nearly all of the sites lack stone tools, but have mammoth bones that seem to have been processed into tools. The evidence against these bones breaking as they did through purely natural forces is persuasive: all of the sites are located in the "lowest-energy geological contexts" possible – in fine, wind-blown sands that couldn't break apart bones (unlike cave ceiling fragments flaking off, as at Brazilian Pedra Furada). The bones were not trampled because the "heavy" bones (such as robust thigh bones) are broken apart while "light" bones (such as ribs) are intact. Nor is there any evidence the bones were eaten and cracked by carnivores. To prove their point, Steve and his team even traveled to Africa and butchered an elephant that had died of natural causes: their experiment was able to replicate almost exactly the ancient tools the Holens are finding, by using a massive rock to pound away at a hulking, stinking, bloody elephant bone.

The Holens' hypothesis is that before 30,000 years ago humans had moved to the eastern edge of Siberia, and sometime before 22,000 years ago they pushed into the New World. These people used a simple stone technology that has been overlooked by generations of scholars. (The 14 identified sites across the Plains lack stone spear points, they believe, because the mammoths there were not hunted, but only scavenged to make a few bone tools.) The Clovis technology that developed by 13,500 years ago represented the much later appearance of a new way of making stone tools, which perhaps emerged in the U.S. Southwest and Mexico and then quickly spread north and south. The Holens believe it is possible that there were multiple waves of migrants from Asia. But most definitely Clovis was not the first at 13,500 years ago.

Still, without unambiguous stone tools, many will question the Holens' work, particularly on account of criterion 2: clear evidence of a human presence. When I asked David Meltzer about Steve's research, he replied that he wasn't familiar with it in detail. But, like Steve, David is eager to follow the evidence wherever it leads; he just thinks the evidence currently leads to around 16,000 years ago. "If the evidence takes us back further, I am okay with that, so long as the evidence withstands critical scrutiny," he told me. "There is no such thing as a free pre-Clovis lunch!"

Steve Holen, now retired, isn't looking for a free lunch. He's looking for answers while he can. "I just really want to know a better answer to this question before I croak," he laughed. "I don't spend a lot of time worrying if other people accept this research. It's like any kind of quest. It lasts a lifetime."

Although no single recent site has definitively decided the issue of America's antiquity, in just the last few years the "Clovis First" model has become increasingly untenable. In 2011, an article in the premier journal *Science* offered evidence of a site near Austin, Texas, containing thousands of fragments of stone tools; the oldest dates are 15,500 years ago. The next year, again in *Science*, came another report of a pre-Clovis cultural tradition, found in Paisley Caves, Oregon: a human coprolite (that is, fossilized poop), preserved in the dryness of a cave, dating to 14,340 years ago. Now, instead of just five possible sites being identified as pre-Clovis, as in 1988, Paulette Steeves, a Ph.D. student who has worked with Steve Holen, has, although controversially, identified more than 400 across North, Central, and South America.

The 13,500-year barrier has been broken. But as a result the picture of the origins of the first Americans is arguably fuzzier than when the Folsom point was uncovered in 1927. The historical map tracing the Clovis pioneers has been erased. Archaeologists are left holding a blank sheet of paper – both the Native American past and their field's future waiting to be redrawn.

If you want to pick a fight with an American archaeologist, then utter the word "Solutrean." It's been a fighting word for well over a century. As far back as the 1870s, archaeologists hypothesized that Paleolithic people came to the Americas not from the east but the west. Over time, even as the Asia-America connection became increasingly clear, a small fringe of scholars continued to be curious about similarities between the stone tool technology that made up the Clovis culture and an ancient human culture in France and Iberia known as the Solutrean. In particular, the Clovis and Solutrean traditions, although separated by thousands of miles and thousands of years, seemed to many to have strikingly similar spear-points, chipped out of stone into finger-length blades as sleek as missiles.

While Steve Holen is challenging the orthodoxy of the timing of the first migration, others are challenging the consensus about its place of origin. In 2004, two archaeologists published a paper entitled "The North Atlantic Ice-Edge Corridor: A Possible Paleolithic Route to the New World." Bruce Bradley (a professor at the University of Exeter in England) and Denis

Stanford (a curator at the Smithsonian's National Museum of Natural History) argued that the "exclusive focus" on a Bering Straits migration "has not been productive." Instead, they claimed that two decades of evidence now indicate that the origins of the Clovis culture could be traced to migrants from Europe, sometime between 19,000 and 26,000 years ago. This paper, later expanded into more articles and a popular but controversial 2012 book, *Across Atlantic Ice: The Origin of America's Clovis Culture*, begins by dismantling the notion that the Bering Straits explanation is based on good science. "These ideas on New World origins," they write, "are based on informed speculation and are not supported by archaeological evidence." The Bering Straits theory, they assert, "has become dogma, and ultimately ideology." Bradley and Stanford insist: "the origin of Clovis culture and technology remain a mystery."

Extraordinary claims require extraordinary evidence. Bradley and Stanford begin by addressing the unknowns about the Clovis cultural tradition. They emphasize the peculiar lack of Clovis sites in Alaska, and the lack of an obvious pre-Clovis-like culture in Siberia. They accept some research that suggests Beringia was "essentially blocked" by uninhabitable glaciers between 11,000 and 22,000 years ago, and deride another hypothesis, for lack of direct evidence, that Clovis hunters arrived in boats across the Bering Sea. In contrast, the authors argue that the Solutrean tradition is older than the Clovis tradition and thus a viable candidate as a precursor. When they consider the stone tool technology of the two cultures – looking at features such as "overshot flaking" (that is, in the process of thinning a stone spear-point with a hammer tool, a flake of stone is intentionally broken off that travels across the entire point, from one edge to another) – they believe the "degree of similarity is astounding." After listing a half-dozen shared technologies, Bradley and Stanford admit that one or two methods could have been independently invented, "but a duplication of the complete comprehensive technological system seems unlikely to have occurred without a historical connection."

The hypothesis Bradley and Stanford propose would revise world history. They suggest that as massive ice sheets moved south from the Arctic about 26,000 years ago, people in southern Europe followed rich sea-resources and newly-forming broad plains filled with tasty mammals in a northwesterly direction, until they "inevitably" entered the new continent. "Some families eventually established camps along the Western Atlantic seaboard," they envision as the most likely scenario, "and did not return."

With their push for the Solutrean hypothesis, Bradley and Stanford have received equal measures of fame and fury. Nearly every leading Paleoindian archaeologist has challenged the North Atlantic theory. Their arguments have been many. They range from the observation that there are perhaps more differences than similarities between Solutrean and Clovis stone technology, and that, given the very nature of making stone tools, convergence (coming up with similar solutions in different places) is to be expected; to the documented art tradition found in Paleolithic Europe (think of the ethereal cave-paintings adorning Lascaux), but the lack of it in Clovis-age sites; to the point that there is little to no skeletal, dental, or linguistic evidence; and to the evidence that the North Atlantic 20,000 years ago would have been inhospitable. Even the apparent technical similarity between the two stone-point traditions is misleading. In a key 2013 paper, published in the *Journal of Archaeological Science*, a brilliant young scholar named Metin Erin and his colleagues show that the so-called "overshot flaking" almost certainly represents "accidental products" of the process used to create spear-points. Many also note that a problematic gap of 5,000 years separates the end of the Solutrean culture and the beginning of the Clovis tradition.

In the last few years yet another line of evidence has radically reshaped our view of the first Americans – DNA. In 2008, a Danish evolutionary biologist named Eske Willerslev entered the global elite of super-star scientists by developing new techniques to decode the DNA from ancient humans. Based on the remains of three people – in Oregon, Montana, and Siberia – Willerslev has developed a hypothesis that sometime before 24,000 years ago, a group of East Asians split off and moved north into the Siberian wilderness. There they met a different group who had traveled eastward from the Steppes of Europe. The two groups blended; eventually, sometime before 14,000 years ago, their offspring migrated east across Beringia into North America becoming one of the founding populations for Native Americans. Willerslev's results have invalidated both the Solutrean hypothesis and the "Clovis First" model.

Roger Echo-Hawk doesn't look like a rabble-rouser. He looks more like the self-described hippie he once was, and still is. His brown hair, streaked with strands of gray, is worn long, parted in the middle, with a thin braid on one side. When we recently sat down together in a sun-filled atrium at the Denver Museum of Nature and Science, Roger slipped off his sandals and folded his bare feet underneath him. But within minutes of talking, as he launched into some of his most radical ideas, his laidback air was replaced by intense animation. Roger was arguing that oral traditions – the spoken stories told by tribal communities over the generations – could contain remembrances of historical events 40,000 years old. Roger is challenging how we know about the past by suggesting that Native American traditions retain memories of the very dawn of human civilization.

Roger Echo-Hawk is a historian by training, and by nature, with a long interest in the history of his tribe – the Pawnee Nation, with a reservation today in Oklahoma. In the 1980s, his lawyer brother Walter Echo-Hawk became the country's leading figure in the fight to get sacred objects and skeletons returned from museums. Roger was recruited as a consultant to help study which human remains in museums collections were ancestral to the Pawnee. He decided that he would use all available information, including oral traditions. As he began to study these narratives, many of which were written down by anthropologists in the late 1800s, he was struck by how many elders spoke about his tribe's distant origins. Yet the language used seemed as if the storytellers were relating not some mythical epoch, but rather specific, real events. What if, Roger began to wonder, Native American oral tradition "preserves glimpses and echoes of the long-vanished" Paleolithic world?

When he entered graduate school at the University of Colorado at Boulder to pursue a master's degree in history, he learned that scholars had no set limit on how long oral traditions go back in time. Many claimed 100 years as an upper limit; more daring scholars pushed it to 4,000 years. Roger reasoned that early human parents would have needed to convey important information for survival to their children – such as the fact that sex leads to children, how to make stone tools, what plants to eat – who in turn would have told their children. Roger came to believe that the durability of oral traditions reached back to the beginnings of "sustained social complexity," which many anthropologists place around 40,000 years ago.

Who are we? Where did we come from? Roger knew that these are some of the most basic questions humans ask themselves. "These questions didn't start with writing, but go back long ago," he told me. Remembering one's origins was perhaps included in this set of survival heirlooms, the first knowledge purposefully passed between the generations. Roger finds it absurd to imagine that early humans did not talk about their lives and tell their children stories. In contrast, most archaeologists write about "past peoples as if they were actors in silent movies."

In graduate school, Roger first worked with Vine Deloria Jr., a political radical turned professor, a member of the Oglala Sioux and one of archaeology's most outspoken critics. In 1995, in his book *Red Earth, White Lies*, Deloria articulated a kind of Indian Creationism constructed from oral traditions, in which Native peoples emerged from the earth itself in the Americas. He argued that archaeologists had created a fiction in Beringia; the Arctic land bridge between Siberia and Alaska, Deloria said, never existed at all.

But rather than backing away from archaeology like Deloria, Roger rushed towards it. He was struck by the similarities between how many Native American oral traditions start "in the geographic context of a place of darkness," while winter darkness is one of the Arctic's defining features. Many scholars interpret the emergence from darkness as a metaphor for a time before time itself began (often phrased as "time immemorial") – or as an allegory for how all of us begin life enveloped in the unknown, made from the stardust of the cosmos in the dark slumber of our mothers' wombs.

Roger acknowledged that these are powerful metaphors that would have resonated with his ancestors. But what if the metaphor was just a vehicle to remember real events? He began to develop a theory he called the "principle of memorability," which predicts that real history endures embedded in oral tradition *because* it is told in a way that is memorable.

"We were told by old people that our people came out from the ground," begins one origin story, told in 1903 to an anthropologist by James R. Murie, a member of the Skidi band of Pawnee. Roger closely examined this narrative. After emergence, the people are met by a spirit-being named Mother-Corn who helped lead the way. At first the people must flee wild creatures "until they came to a chasm which they could not cross." With the help of the Badger, the people began to cross only to confront the next obstacle: "wide, thick ice and deep water." After beseeching different animals for help, finally the Loon drove the ice and water away. "There was now dry land," the episode ends, "so that the people crossed over." They then completed their journey to their homeland on the Great Plains.

In a 2000 article published in the journal *American Antiquity*, Roger argued that the "dark origin point ... can be interpreted as an ancient memory of the Arctic Circle and the Beringian homeland of the people who settled in North America." His principle of memorability explains that this history has been "distorted" over time because "a strict historical account of Beringia would serve a less useful purpose than the more memorable story of an underworld that opens conveniently upon a particular homeland."

Several years ago, Roger and I sat down for coffee at the Denver Museum with David Meltzer. In a friendly but animated conversation, Roger expressed his frustration that Meltzer's important book *First Peoples in a New World* examines a range of evidence – archaeological, genetic, linguistic, biological – while reducing the potential contribution of oral tradition to a single line in a footnote. In his defense, David explained that he found Roger's theory fascinating, but, like most archaeologists, he studies Indians past, not present; he doesn't have the expertise to analyze Roger's provocative ideas nor, he added, is there yet established scholarship examining collective memory from the Pleistocene on which he could draw.

Roger admitted as much. "Even I'm not an expert on the oral traditions in deep time," he confessed to me, adding, "Because no one is. There are no academic departments that specialize in this. No conferences. No major books." His goal in this work has been to suggest at least the possibility that oral traditions can contribute to our understanding of the origins of the America's first people. "Even if my ideas are half-baked," he said, "there will be other bakers! I wanted to put everything out there." Still, he finds it exasperating that other scholars haven't picked up on what he believes to be an untapped source of vital knowledge. "The responsibility of the scholar," Roger told me, "is to create insights based on exploring the evidence as conscientiously as possible. So what is the evidence? Most scholars of the Ice Age have simply decided that oral traditions are not credible. That's what needs to change."

Unlike Vine Deloria Jr., who was an Indian creationist, Roger told me that he has been accused of being an Indian nationalist – that he is trying to promote an agenda of racial bonding for American Indians by proving their traditions are true. The accusation strikes me as empty. Like most of his colleagues Roger wants nothing more than to follow the truth – even if it leads to strikingly unorthodox, unpopular conclusions. He insists that his goals are lofty.

"When I think about people and ancient history, my ultimate feeling is that there is an interesting story to tell about what our ancestors handed down," Roger told me, growing excited. "Part of what they handed down was these threads from the very deep past, stories handed down by many generations. What an incredible achievement!" He paused. "Maybe I do history because I love finding how little pieces of a puzzle fit together. But the more we know about our humanity, the more ways we have of being human. The more we know about our humanity, the more ways we have of envisioning what we want for ourselves and our descendants in the future. So to me it's all about enriching our sense of self and building mutual respect among people – this sense of the expansiveness of our humanity."

Not long ago, I visited the Folsom kill site with a small group led by David Eck, an archaeologist with the New Mexico State Land Office. In a convoy of cars, we passed through the town of Folsom, a few dilapidated houses, then drove through a ranch gate, passing grazing cattle and pronghorn, and parked on a grassy knoll, overlooking a green, graceful valley. The day was warmed by a late summer sun, tempered by scattered, pillowy clouds. We signed a form promising not to sue the New Mexico State Land Office if we died in the next few hours, and then hiked about a mile, up and down hills, until we arrived at a steep ledge overlooking Wild Horse Draw.

The Folsom kill site looks like any anonymous desert creek. No neatly cut excavation pits. No monument. No memorial or exhibit, although we were told that a highway marker was shot out long ago. In single file, we walked into the creek bed, thick with willow shoots and orange and purple wildflowers. The mud stuck to my shoes. David Eck encouraged us to look for fragments of ancient bison against one sloping wall of the creek, but I couldn't find a fossil. We walked back to the cars.

Several hours later, as the day cooled into evening, we parked at the edge of a cemetery. Low gravestones were scattered, encircled by a barbed wire fence. Our tour had one last stop. "George was buried at the back of the cemetery," David explained to me. "Then they rerouted the highway and moved the gate. Now he's the first one you see!" We chuckled at the irony. Still, the privilege is modest. The grave is covered in weeds. At its head is an unadorned granite headstone: "George McJunkin, 1856–1922."

The vacant creek and weed-choked grave made me reflect that Folsom should be more properly honored, for this was the site that became the threshold where centuries of conjecture were left behind and a new age of discovery emerged. But the fact is that Folsom has been eclipsed by more important sites, by claims of more distant times, by more intriguing geographies of origins, by more novel methods. We've learned so much since 1927, driven by archaeology's florescence as a discipline and the revolutions in the science of Paleoindian history. We now know in concrete detail about the intrepid bands of first Americans who traversed the Ice Age with little more than their intelligence, who survived through the millennia to establish the human story of our continent.

And yet, 88 years after Folsom, it is striking how little we still know. Although an ancient migration from Europe is unlikely, the exact location (beyond Asia) and exact time (beyond 13,500 years ago) continue to elude us. Finds like those by Steve Holen appear just as fuzzy as those first stone tools that inspired the idea of the *palaios* age, while inventive methods, like Roger Echo-Hawk's bid to hear the voices from the deep past, leave most archaeologists unsure of their own field's potential. It is impressive how many questions about the first Americans remain to be answered.

George McJunkin, too, should not be forgotten so soon. Given the field's oscillations, archaeology could use inspiration from the black cowboy – his drive, passion, curiosity, and rejection of the status quo. He seems to have appreciated that history does not reveal itself, that the past has to be pursued and fashioned from the fragile clues of broken bones and stones. Perhaps, too, a little of George's luck could rub off on archaeologists, the kind of wild luck that depends on a passing summer storm pausing too long over the headwaters of a desert river.

— 5 —

Remembering Slack Farm

A. Gwynn Henderson

Aerial view of Slack Farm shortly after the looters were indicted. (Photo by David Pollack, used with permission.)

It's been nearly 28 years since the lives of my husband and myself were irrevocably changed by what has euphemistically been referred to as "the Slack Farm Incident." Before, during, and – for several years after fieldwork ended at that looted ancient Native American village site in Union County, Kentucky – our lives were consumed by Slack Farm. At the height of fieldwork, we couldn't open a local newspaper without seeing an article about Slack Farm. We couldn't talk to anyone, once they discovered we were involved with the project, without being grilled. What was new in the case? Had the looters been sent to jail yet? What kinds of artifacts had we found? What were the Indians doing? How can I help?

Everything about Slack Farm broke the mold. The diversity of circumstances, people, and events surrounding the looting, the resultant archaeological study, and the subsequent outcomes set that project apart from all the others I have been involved in, before or since, over the course of my over 40-year-long archaeological career. In the extent of the looters' damage. In the involvement of lawyers and police. In the response by Native peoples to the grave desecration. In the amount of public involvement to right the wrong. In the site's visibility in the media. And especially, in the project's long-lasting impact on archaeology and on heritage law: the information it produced about ancient Native farming peoples, the repercussions it set in motion, and the legacies it left behind. From start to finish, my husband and a good friend were co-directors of the project, and close friends were members of the field crew. As for me, to have witnessed the destruction first-hand and to have been involved in so many aspects of the project: that was life-changing.

The Slack Farm Incident began with a phone call in November 1987. But in truth, it had begun decades earlier, when a childhood hobby turned from passion to obsession.

December 19, 1987: David Pollack's 36th birthday. On a gray, bone-cold morning, Pollack (an archaeologist with the Kentucky Heritage Council) and David Wolf (the Kentucky State Forensic Anthropologist) were riding in a Kentucky State police car on their way to conduct a damage assessment of a site in Union County called Slack Farm. The short drive from the airport in Henderson, Kentucky took them across the rolling ridge-tops of Henderson and adjacent Union counties, then past agricultural fields and coal tipples, before the road dropped down into the broad Ohio River floodplain. Farmers had harvested their crops of corn and soybeans: now the ground was clear, or nearly so, and Indian relic collectors could return to walk the fields in search of spear points and arrowheads.

The Kentucky Heritage Council is the State Historic Preservation Office, the state agency responsible for documenting important cultural resources. Although Pollack was just beginning his fifth year at the Council, he had nearly a decade of archaeological fieldwork under his belt. He was no stranger to the impacts of looting and vandalism on archaeological sites. In late November, several weeks before the site visit, Pollack received a call from a western Kentucky resident: men were digging graves on the old Slack Farm property. Since it was unlawful to dig up human remains in Kentucky, Pollack informed David Wolf, the man responsible for attending to human remains, ancient or modern, in the Commonwealth. Wolf called the Henderson State Police Post and asked them to check out the story. The Post's captain sent Sergeant Miles Hart. Hart was a reformed looter who knew all about the allure of digging and was well aware of the ancient Indian site on the farm. As Hart approached the site, he was met by several of the looters, who informed him he was trespassing and demanded he leave. A few hours later, Hart returned to the site with a warrant and a cease-and-desist order. The men were later charged with grave robbing and were arrested.

In the weeks after the arrest, Pollack met with David Morgan, the Director of the Kentucky Heritage Council, Cheryl Ann Munson of Indiana University, and the Kentucky archaeological community to discuss the appropriate course of action to take. Those conversations had culminated in this mid-December visit by Wolf and Pollack. Pollack would look back on this trip as a watershed moment, a turning point in Ohio Valley archaeology.

Locals had known about the Indian site on the Slack Family's farm for decades. As early as 1871, Sydney Lyons had mentioned it in a brief survey report filed with the Smithsonian Institution. Oddly enough, Pollack had only recently read about Slack Farm during his review of a research proposal Munson had submitted to the Heritage Council. Munson had conducted research at ancient farming village sites in Indiana and wanted to extend her work across the Ohio River into Kentucky. Among the sites in Henderson and Union counties she planned to visit was Site 15UN28 – the designation assigned to Slack Farm by the University of Kentucky's Office of State Archaeology.

Thus, on December 19, 1987, all Pollack knew about 15UN28 was this: sometime after A.D. 1400, above the active Ohio River floodplain near the mouth of Sibley Creek, Native American farmers had lived in a village for at least several decades and had buried their dead within it. The remains of their village took the form of dark soil and thousands of artifacts – an indelible mark on this modern agricultural field. But the looters, too, had left their own indelible marks.

Nearly every farm field in Kentucky holds fragments of its indigenous past: most commonly chips of flint, broken scrapers, spear points, and arrowheads, but sometimes pottery fragments, bits of animal bone or shell, and rarely, smoking-pipes and bone ornaments. And it's no wonder: Kentucky's Indian history is 12,000 years long, making it the Commonwealth's longest historical period.

Most kids in rural areas grow up walking plowed fields, picking up spear points from their family's or neighbors' farm fields, and keeping their collections safe in cigar boxes. They open the boxes from time to time to examine the contents, remembering where they found their favorites and conjuring up visions of ancient battles. Most leave all that behind with their childhood, but a few become consumed with finding, owning, buying, selling, and trading Indian relics of all kinds: stone tools, exquisite shell and bone ornaments, animal-shaped stone smoking-pipes, whole ceramic jars and bowls, and human bones. Switching the cigar boxes of their youth for basements lined with display cases, the most fanatical put up separate buildings – private museums, really – to house their collections. Some even make a living buying and selling artifacts. For these individuals, walking plowed fields to find pieces to add to their collections is no longer enough. They *have* to dig and, in so doing, they cross the line from interested lay people to looters, from law-abiding citizens to criminals.

In the summer of 1987, two local men approached William D. Lambert, the new owner of Mrs. Slack's farm, for permission to dig on his property. Mrs. Slack had not permitted digging, but she was gone now. Her death signaled an opportunity to make money and the promise of collectible, marketable artifacts. The men took it.

Owning an archaeological site is a double-edged sword. Possessing a piece of the past can be a joy, the stewardship responsibilities, a burden; Lambert saw only the burden. Looters sneaking onto the site had left large holes on his property, a safety hazard in the summer when the farmers who leased the property drove their combines through the field. This was a problem that was not going away. Lambert also saw an opportunity when the two men approached him for permission to dig. For him, it was a way to unload his burden and make some money in the process. Naïvely, he figured that if the looters robbed all of the burials, nothing would remain – problem solved. Lambert said yes. At the price of $10,000, the men could dig on his farm for six months, from the Fall of 1987 to the Spring of 1988. The lease specified that up to 12 individuals could be on the site at any one time, that they could dig as long as they did not break any laws, and that they could keep whatever they found; when their time was up, their "digging rights" would cease. The two men paid Lambert's asking price, then sold shares to ten others, who each paid $1000 for the right to dig. Thus, even before the first shovel was raised, the two men had recouped their investment.

The Ohio River is wide as its swings by Union County on its trip to join the Mississippi River at Cairo, Illinois. It parts briefly at Wabash Island, which sits at the mouth of Indiana's Wabash River. Slack Farm lies opposite the mouth, on the Ohio's southern shore, at the center of the homeland of the Caborn-Welborn people. From the A.D. 1400s to the early A.D. 1700s, Caborn-Welborn villages, both large and small, dotted the floodplain on both sides of the Ohio River in a 60-mile stretch of the valley from Evansville, Indiana downstream to the mouth of the Saline River. Sprinkled among the villages were hamlets and tiny farmsteads.

The ancestors of the Caborn-Welborn people had lived in this region for a very long time. Outside of what is now Evansville, they had built their major town and mound center at Angel Mounds not long after A.D. 1000. Networks of social and political relationships linked the chiefs at Angel to chiefs living in similar town and mound centers across the Southeastern U.S. and the Midwest. These networks provided the Angel chiefs with the knowledge and the ritual items they needed to be successful leaders.

For reasons unknown, many of these farming cultures and most of the chiefly networks collapsed around A.D. 1400. So, too, did the farming culture centered at Angel Mounds. Thus, Caborn-Welborn history begins with the collapse of their grandparents' way of life. In A.D. 1400, the Caborn-Welborn people faced many of the same challenges the people of Europe faced in the wake of World War II: namely, to build a new world from the rubble of the old. Caborn-Welborn people continued many of their ancestors' traditions. Farming corn, beans, and squash was their mainstay; hunting, gathering, and fishing rounded out their diet. They built permanent, mud-walled houses and buried their dead in nearby cemeteries. However, Caborn-Welborn leaders were unable to muster the political power and influence of their grandfathers; there would be no large, flat-topped platform mounds for them to live on. Quite literally, they would not achieve the heights of their forefathers.

In this new world, Caborn-Welborn leaders expanded long-distance trading connections with different sorts of people living to the south and north.

These connections provided them with objects made from exotic materials, like marine shell, catlinite (a soft, carvable red stone native to southeastern Minnesota), and metal. Grieving families often placed these highly-prized objects with the dead. Caborn-Welborn leaders and the people who followed them created a viable and prosperous culture that endured for over 300 years. And their largest village was Slack Farm.

The police car turned onto the farm road and headed toward the site, past the silos and toward the barn where Hart had nailed up the cease-and-desist order weeks before. The barn would become a reference point for volunteers like me in the months ahead.

"I don't know if this is illegal, but it is definitely wrong," Pollack recalls a seasoned trooper saying during that December visit. Some of the most intensely looted areas at the site were in the vicinity of the barn. The men immediately noted the remains of infants, children, and adults scattered about. Skulls sat on dirt piles. I remember the look on my husband's face as he described to me what he had seen: "It's a good thing you didn't come with us: all you would have done is cry."

Weeks later, I did see it with my own eyes, and he was right: I wept at the destruction. Even now, remembering, it is hard to find words to describe the scene, and they cannot convey the emotional impact. I felt frustrated and helpless. "What's to be done, now?" I thought. "Filling the holes back in and documenting what's happened can *never* put it back as it was." I felt anger – such intense anger. For a long time, history had lain there, undisturbed. Then, in an instant, the looters had ripped it to shreds. I wanted to scream at them: "How could you *do* this? No artifact is worth this destruction!" But they were not present to listen – only the evidence of their work was. Holes. Piles of dirt. Broken jars. Desecrated graves.

The scale of destruction was enormous. The field was pockmarked with 450 holes, scattered across about 15 acres. The most concentrated looting was located within a seven-acre area in front of the barn, but the holes and the dirt piles adjacent to them were not the worst of it. In their haste to find graves containing marine shell gorgets, catlinite pipes, and copper pendants, the looters had also dug through house floors, hearths, and storage pits, recklessly destroying the record of past lives and the evidence that Caborn-Welborn people had lived at this place. Broken pottery, arrowheads, charred corncobs, and animal bones littered the ground.

Pollack, Wolf, and the troopers walked for a couple of hours that day, attempting to process what they saw before starting to collect evidence. This was proving to be a very different site visit than previous ones Pollack had made to looted sites. Exactly *how* different a visit it was, he could not have known.

The depth of callous disrespect for the dead was overwhelming. The looters had used shovels but also had brought in small bobcats to use when they needed to move larger amounts of backdirt. Their work was not done in secret, at night by flashlight; after all, they had permission, and so could work unchallenged in broad daylight. They systematically mined the site for the objects lovingly placed, ostensibly for eternity, in the graves of the departed. The looters soon learned that the villagers had laid out their dead in rows in distinct cemeteries. Once the looters hit one grave – quite literally, "pay-dirt" – they knew others would be nearby. One of the men did not like the skulls of the people whose graves he was looting staring at him while he dug, and so he routinely used his shovel to shave off the faces and toss them out of the pit.

Eventually, Pollack, Wolf, and the troopers turned to the work at hand, doing their best to conduct a preliminary damage assessment, taking photographs and collecting evidence. At the end of their visit, they had recovered the remains of 34 individuals and sufficient evidence to charge the looters with 34 counts of desecrating graves. In the eight weeks the looters had worked before they were arrested, they had turned an unremarkable agricultural field into a war zone, a moonscape, a desecration. Why had they dug for so long before anyone noticed? For so long without public outcry? Because to the looters, Slack Farm was only an Indian burial ground and the people in those graves were not important.

From the very beginning, Native people were involved at Slack Farm, and this involvement was another aspect that set the site apart. In 1987, American Indians faced many challenges – poverty, alcoholism, access to education and adequate healthcare – but they were beginning to find their common voice and speak out, exercising their political muscle. An especially emotional issue was the desecration of Indian graves that was taking place all across the United States, and the thousands of boxes of Indian bones held in American museums.

Dennis Banks, an activist leader, teacher, and author, was living in northern Kentucky when reports of the looting at Slack Farm began to surface. An Anishinabe, Banks worked on the national stage for Indian causes and Indian rights and was, at that time, best known for co-founding the American Indian Movement (AIM) and leading the 1973 occupation of Wounded Knee on the Pine Ridge Indian Reservation. In the months ahead, Banks would play an important role at Slack Farm, serving as one of the major American Indian spokespeople during the events following the looting.

When Banks remembers what he saw at Slack Farm, he is visibly moved. He speaks of feeling physically ill because of the extent and magnitude of the destruction at the site and the deep, emboldened disregard and disrespect for Indian people it represented. Many Native people shared Banks' response.

With the recovery of the evidence, Slack Farm was now a crime scene. The State needed to collect additional evidence from the site to continue with criminal proceedings against the looters. Specifically, it needed to determine how many Native American graves they had desecrated. There were research questions to be answered, too – Who were these people whose village and graves the looters had destroyed? – but questions would have to take a back seat to the criminal investigation.

By February, Pollack and Munson had formulated a plan of how to proceed. The task ahead of them was enormous, but straightforward. To support evidence collection, the Heritage Council allowed Munson to redirect her grant funds to the case, and it awarded grant monies to the University of Kentucky to assist. University of Kentucky bioarchaeologist and Anthropology Museum director Dr. Mary Lucas Powell agreed to supervise the analysis of the human skeletal remains. Between them, Munson and Pollack had nearly a half century of archaeological field experience at diverse site types in a variety of settings. They would jointly direct the day-to-day site operations. Five experienced archaeologists from Indiana University and the University of Kentucky joined the project as permanent crew members. As capable as they were, however, Pollack and Munson knew this crew would not be enough. They would need volunteer labor.

In 1987, unlike today, volunteering to work on an archaeological site in the Ohio Valley was uncommon. The number of people who had damaged the site and its graves had been small – 12 men, more or less, working continuously for almost two months. The number of people it would take to undo their desecration was 50 times that. So, Pollack and Munson scheduled the work-week from Thursday to Monday to accommodate volunteers. Then the calls went out.

People heard about the site and wanted to help. Over the course of fieldwork alone, some 500 people volunteered. They came from many walks of life and from all across the region. Retired IBM executives. College students. Local citizens. Girl Scout troops. Professional archaeologists from Kentucky and surrounding states. One woman came so often, she got to pick where she worked on the site. A mother and her home-schooled son came nearly every week for a day or two. Some volunteers became regular crew members. In time, Pollack and Munson assigned them to special tasks as befitted their skills: Pat Ritz, for instance, became the team's burial cleaning specialist, and a retiree was given the responsibility for bagging and proveniencing artifacts.

Archaeologists were uniquely qualified to recover the evidence for the case against the Slack Farm looters, for like detectives, archaeologists, too, collect "evidence" about peoples' lives. They are trained to read the soil and to recognize artifacts. Archaeologists feel soil changes with their trowels. Drawing on experience gained at other sites, they can anticipate and recognize patterns. They dig square holes, not round ones. They do not dig indiscriminately, keeping only the pretty artifacts. They meticulously excavate with shovel, trowel, and brush, screening the soil, taking care to label each bag of artifacts so they know exactly where the artifacts came from. Taking notes and photographs, making maps, and recording and organizing all their observations are what archaeologists do. Pollack and Munson wanted to apply all these standard archaeological methods at Slack Farm, but they knew they could not. Their objective was first and foremost to collect evidence in a criminal investigation.

Slack Farm presented Pollack and Munson with challenges few American archaeologists had experienced prior to that time: digging out and documenting looters' holes to collect evidence. The site also represented a strange reverse situation – the holes had already been dug. There were backdirt piles, but the soil in them was unscreened. Some objects had been removed, but no one knew what or from where. Above all, there were no maps or notes, no forms that recorded what had been encountered. Munson and Pollack and their team brought their experience to this mayhem, and order to it all: each hole got its own number, and an adjacent pile was linked to its hole by the same number and a letter.

Looking back on it now, I remember how odd it felt not to spend the time I'd ordinarily spend excavating and documenting a hearth, a trash pit, a house floor. At Slack Farm, the drill was this: presented with a hole, your job was to clean it out, and that meant removing all the loose soil to find the end of the looters' destruction. Perhaps, if the soil had been freshly disturbed, this job would have been easy, but by the time evidence collection began, some holes had been open to the elements for six months. Rain had washed the backdirt piles. The sides of some holes had slumped inward, like wounds drawing closed in healing. Throw the disturbed soil, shovelful by shovelful, into a nearby screen; pit-mates screen the soil, putting artifacts in one bag, human bone in the other. Given the density of materials in some parts of the site, buckets substituted for bags. Once cleaned out and ready for a photograph, the empty hole revealed some of what the looters had destroyed there: edges of storage pits, the bases of hearths, lines of posts (the housewalls) and what the looters had left undisturbed in the graves: half a leg, a torso. Take notes. Move on to the adjacent pile of soil the looters had deposited. Screen the soil, often into an adjacent already-documented hole. Buckets and buckets and buckets of bone. The permanent crew did most of the mapping, on strange-looking graph paper selected purposely for ease in drafting circular features.

The fieldwork started in February and lasted into May. There was snow, frost, sun, and rain. Each day brought another media representative. Media coverage was fierce, especially in the western Kentucky-southwestern Indiana-southeastern Illinois tri-state area. Radio, television, and newspapers focused a constant spotlight on Slack Farm. The site garnered national attention, too, appearing in *Time* magazine while fieldwork was in progress, and in *Archaeology* magazine and *National Geographic* not long after it concluded.

Boxes of bones and artifacts steadily accumulated, each one assigned a unique inventory number – physical testimony to the damage that had occurred. Mounting too, were the field notes. By the end, they would fill 11 bulging binders – maps, lists, descriptions, and hunches waiting to be verified or disproved by the analysis that would take place in the decade ahead.

Was the magnitude of the desecration of Indian graves at Slack Farm a tipping point in the minds of Native individuals like Dennis Banks: "Enough is enough: this must stop"? In the wider scheme of things, after all, the damage done by the Slack Farm looters was no worse than looter impacts to burial grounds throughout the Ohio valley or in the Puebloan Southwest. Or was it because Slack Farm was located east of the Mississippi River, in a region not commonly associated with looting on this scale? Was it because of the media coverage? Was it because of Native peoples' growing confidence to speak out and take action against the injustices they had endured for centuries? Whatever the impetus, the Native American community responded *en masse* to the disrespect the Slack Farm looters had shown toward indigenous people and the graves of their ancestors. Native peoples wanted the looters prosecuted and the bones reburied.

It is important to remember that in 1987, Indian-archaeologist partnerships were rare in the U.S. They were even rarer in Kentucky, one of the few states that lack Indian reservations, a state that, until recently, routinely taught its children that Native peoples never lived in Kentucky permanently, but only hunted there. Linking living Native peoples to the human bones the looters had tossed out of the way was not what Kentucky's citizens would have done at that time.

NAGPRA, the Native American Graves Protection and Repatriation Act, would not arrive to compel such partnerships until 1990. Dialogue is common practice now; but back then it was not, and the call for the reburial of the bones was controversial. The bones were evidence that had to be collected and analyzed for the case against the men. The Indian representatives agreed that this work needed to be done, but they were concerned about how long it would take before the remains could be reinterred at the site.

In the end, what was decided was unusual. There would be a Native presence during fieldwork at Slack Farm. Native people occasionally would lead ceremonies at the site and make offerings of tobacco, song, and prayers, and sometimes the archaeologists could join them. Considered unclean because they were working among disturbed graves, everyone – archaeologists, volunteers, even visitors – and all the boxes of bones were periodically "smudged" by reverently passing a small bundle of smoking sage over person and box alike.

After four months of fieldwork, ceremonies, media attention, and volunteer support, the last hole was cleaned out and documented; the last backdirt pile was screened. The most visible phase, truly the shortest phase of the Slack Farm project, had concluded. But Pollack and Munson now faced a mountain of documents and boxes. They had to sort it all out: both for the criminal investigation and for the archaeological research.

Their first challenge was to get everything washed and sorted. In the field, it is hard to determine whether dirt-covered objects, especially small ones, are fragments of bone or pottery, or even stone. The University of Kentucky's archaeology lab at that time was in the American Building, a rambling, former tobacco warehouse, its lower level covering a couple thousand square feet; it was perfect for the task of processing and analyzing the Slack Farm artifacts. Again, the project depended on the aid of volunteers. To encourage participation, Pollack instituted "Slack Farm Wash Night": every Wednesday night, folks gathered at the lab from 6 to 9 p.m., to wash and sort artifacts. Scores of UK students and community volunteers, especially members of local amateur archaeological societies, spent more than three years washing and sorting the millions of artifacts recovered from the site.

Astonishingly, in 1987, it was only a misdemeanor to disturb graves in Kentucky. But at least in Kentucky, a grave was considered any place where someone was buried – marked or unmarked, regardless of biological or ethnic affiliation, it didn't matter. In neighboring states, it was not illegal to disturb unmarked graves. And in some states, even if marked, graves older than a certain date that were not located in a perpetual-care cemetery deserved no protection. The sobering truth was that, in the neighboring states of Indiana and Illinois, and in most other states, what the men did at Slack Farm would not have been illegal.

In the end, the fact that the men had been charged with breaking Kentucky laws did not matter. Someone has to be willing to prosecute. The Commonwealth's Attorney for Union County was reluctant to pursue the case. He did not consider the destruction of the ancient cemeteries at Slack Farm a punishable offense. It was also deeply frustrating to learn that he had the discretion to turn the case over to the Kentucky Attorney General's office, but chose not to do so. And so the men who looted Slack Farm, although put on probation and prohibited from digging for five years, were never prosecuted.

Pollack and Munson's second challenge was to analyze, write up, and make some sense out of the masses of data collected as part of the criminal investigation. The money they had cobbled together was only to get the evidence out of the ground. After the fieldwork was completed, they had to return to the day-jobs they had put on hold during their response to the crisis. Eventually, they were successful in acquiring funds from the National Endowment for the Humanities to analyze the artifacts, and tell the story of the lives of the people who lived at Slack Farm: to the archaeological community, to the citizens of Kentucky, and beyond. They secured the expertise of specialists to analyze the pottery, the chipped stone, the carbonized plant remains, and the animal bones. They sent samples of burned wood and corn for radiocarbon dating, metal European trade goods to chemists for source analysis, and pottery to specialists in neutron activation analysis for the identification of trade wares.

I had a small hand in this phase of the project, too, helping analyze the pottery and assisting with the analysis of textile impressions on particular vessel forms. I am a ceramic analyst by trade, and the Slack Farm assemblage is, by far, the largest sample of ancient Native American pottery with which I have ever worked. From other sites, I would be lucky to have 20 or 30 fragments large enough to analyze, and I'd squeeze every bit of data I could from the very tiniest diagnostic specimens. The Slack Farm collection consisted of many hundreds of large fragments of every kind of vessel the Caborn-Welborn potters made: jar, bowl, pan, bottle. With a sample like that, I saw the theme, and all the variations on it. It was a delight.

I came to appreciate the diverse techniques the Slack Farm potters used to achieve the look they wanted. There were so many ways to make that beaded rim decoration on hemispherical bowls, to thicken pan rims, to decorate jar necks. I came to recognize the hand of true artists, of master craftsmen, and of serviceable yeomen. I thought of how the people who had used these vessels would have recognized these differences, too, and maybe appreciated the truly well-made examples, as I did.

My introduction to the analysis of the impressions of ancient fabrics on pottery was through my work on the Slack Farm collection. My previous experience had been with cord-marked sherds. Specimens with textile impressions, when present at all, were not very big, and the textiles themselves were not that impressive – a simple basic fabric made from a twisted or "twined" weft over a stationary warp. The world of Caborn-Welborn textiles was another story altogether: impressions of exquisite fabrics with bird's-eye motifs; geometric designs, with stripes of varying widths; broad bands with repeating patterns of zigzags; and dense heavy mats and coarse bags. I suppose, at some level, I knew Native peoples had worn something else besides deerskin leather and furs, but the textile-impressed fabrics on the Slack Farm pottery made it undeniable. The Caborn-Welborn people made and wore clothing decorated in an array of designs and used all kinds of fabrics.

Then, I would remember how it was that I came to be analyzing these artifacts, and it broke my heart. It renewed my disgust for the men who had looted Slack Farm, and who had gotten away with it.

In the end, whatever happened to the men, to the Indians, to the archaeology, to the site? The men who leased digging rights to Slack Farm moved on to other sites, the market in Indian relics ever ready to absorb their "product." It is perhaps justice served that, four years later, some of the men involved in the Slack Farm case were convicted of looting a burial mound in southwestern Indiana and spent some time in jail. In comparison to the enormous destruction they had caused at Slack Farm and at the Indiana mound, I felt it was small consolation, but consolation nevertheless.

Approached by The Archaeological Conservancy to set aside Slack Farm as an archaeological preserve in perpetuity, Lambert showed little interest. His son now owns the site. A move in the late 1990s to list Slack Farm on the National Register of Historic Places failed. That is because listing requires landowner support, and none was forthcoming: indeed, Lambert's son objected.

If measured by these developments alone, it would be hard to see any positive outcomes from the "Slack Farm Incident": no one went to jail, and the site has been afforded no special protection. But there are other ways to measure the impact and legacies of Slack Farm. The positive outcomes were enormous and far-reaching.

Because of Slack Farm, in 1988, Governor Wilkinson and the Kentucky Legislature strengthened Kentucky's laws dealing with the protection of cemeteries. It is now a felony to loot or disturb human remains. Other states soon followed Kentucky's lead. The scale of destruction, the publicity, and the presence of Native Americans at the site during fieldwork raised peoples' awareness of the looting of Indian burial grounds and archaeological sites – in Henderson and Union counties and across the river in Evansville, Indiana; throughout the Ohio Valley; and across the nation.

I believe that the destruction at Slack Farm helped individuals who were working on federal legislation to protect Native American burial grounds and sacred artifacts. Congress passed the Native American Graves Protection and Repatriation Act (NAGPRA) two years after the conclusion of fieldwork at Slack Farm. Controversial at the outset, NAGPRA has opened channels of communication between archaeologists and Native peoples on an unprecedented scale. Because of NAGPRA, the way archaeologists in the U.S. treat human remains and the way American citizens view them has changed, and I think Slack Farm had a hand in that change. Slack Farm is the perfect example to use in teaching historic preservation law (as I found out recently while researching readings for a law enforcement workshop): this Kentucky case brings the ongoing issue of site looting close to home. The project ended years ago, but Pollack and Munson continue to receive requests from authors of books, textbooks, and magazines to use the iconic aerial photo (p. 53) showing the extent of the pockmarked, moonscape of a field.

On a personal level, the archaeological investigation of Slack Farm compelled Pollack, Munson, and me to prepare the first of what would become a series of public-oriented booklets on Kentucky archaeology. Kentucky Educational Television in 1994 produced *A Native Presence*, a documentary that still airs today, highlighting issues surrounding the looting of graves and archaeological sites and examining the Native American presence in Kentucky. State-wide and nationally, Slack Farm prompted the American archaeological community to do a better job of educating the public about the state's and the country's rich archaeological heritage and the need to enlist help in protecting these fragile resources.

The Slack Farm artifacts, notes, photographs, and forms are curated in perpetuity at the William S. Webb Museum of Anthropology on the campus of the University of Kentucky, and the collection is available for researchers to study. The recovered materials became the foundation of Pollack's dissertation research, which was supported by the National Science Foundation, and a subsequent book on the Caborn-Welborn culture. The site assemblage also has been the focus of student theses and papers and public exhibits. There is so much more to learn. The work that has been done to date has only scratched the surface.

And, finally, what of the site itself? Shortly after the completion of fieldwork, the Indians' request was realized: the bones of their ancestors were reburied. Hundreds of boxes holding the remains of over 900 men, women, and children were returned to the site and reinterred in the largest looter holes, as part of a private reburial ceremony overseen by Chief Shenandoah of the Haudenosaunee. Native people return to the site periodically to remember. Despite the intense destruction of the village cemeteries and some of its habitation areas, over ninety percent of this fascinating site remains undisturbed. Today, Slack Farm is an unremarkable Union County agricultural field on a terrace adjacent to the wide Ohio River. Local law enforcement officers occasionally drive by to check up on it – given past events, who would loot it now? There are no markers, no signs, no evidence of what happened there decades ago.

But I remember. And, now, perhaps so will you.

— 6 —

Pot Biographies and Plunder

VERNON SILVER

The Sarpedon krater unveiled in Rome, January 18, 2008. (Photo by Vernon Silver.)

Just after noon on a sunny day in Rome, January 18, 2008, about 100 people – including police, archaeologists, journalists, politicians, lawyers, and bureaucrats – gathered at the headquarters of Italy's attorney general for the unveiling of the Sarpedon krater, which three decades earlier had left the country at the hands of tomb robbers and smugglers, ended up at New York's Metropolitan Museum of Art, and after lengthy negotiations, had just been repatriated. Many of the guests at the unveiling had played some role in winning the return of the 2,500-year-old pot by the painter Euphronios, one of just six known vases that he had signed at the height of his renown in Athens. To each of these guests, this vessel for mixing water and wine meant something different.

The players in the repatriation drama filed into the grand Sala Vanvitelli, a towering, frescoed room bathed in natural sunlight, kissing on cheeks and shaking hands, as the 1 p.m. ceremony approached. The krater itself sat hidden under a white sheet in a corner, on a low-lying wooden table that was covered with a red tablecloth.

General Roberto Conforti, the retired commander of the Carabinieri art police, for whom the krater's return was a law-enforcement victory, mingled with Paolo Ferri, the prosecutor who had won indictments and a conviction for the smuggling of the pot. For the prosecutor, the repatriation was part of a campaign against what he saw as corrupt and immoral museum curators. Anna Maria Moretti Sgubini, the government's chief of Etruscan archaeology, had helped negotiate the deal with the Metropolitan Museum. To her, the vase's meanings were manifold: her father, Mario Moretti, had held the very same post she now occupied at the time when clandestine diggers took the krater from a tomb in Cerveteri in 1971. To the politicians there, the repatriation was local news: a victory for cooperation among the various political parties amid ever-changing governments.

By contrast, the Met's Director, Philippe de Montebello – who stayed home in New York for the occasion – had predicted the Italians would treat the krater as a trophy in a nationalistic victory for retentionist cultural property policies motivated by "nationalism and misplaced patriotism." "I suspect they're more likely to show it initially as a trophy of conquest," he had told *The New York Times* a few days before signing the return agreement in February 2006.

He wasn't entirely wrong. But he also missed a compelling part of what was really at work. Montebello, like many others in the museum business, had become used to understanding demands for repatriation as a game of "Who owns it?" This was the ongoing battle between collectors and museums on one side, and the governments of source countries, such as Italy, Egypt, and Greece, on the other. The line in the sand was about cultural heritage laws, valid bills of sale, and whether civilization was better served by having its treasures in major galleries with millions of annual visitors or in the lands of their archaeological origins. But the scene that afternoon in Rome made it clear that the debate was missing the point. It didn't much matter where the stuff belonged – it mattered where it had *been*.

With the unveiling about to start, Ferri, the prosecutor, took a seat in the front row. Sitting next to him was Giuseppe Proietti, secretary general of the Culture Ministry, and its highest-ranked civilian employee. He had a long history with the krater: as a young archaeologist, the very first excavation he directed was a salvage operation in 1974 at the site of the looting, on land partly owned by Giacomo Medici, the same man who would later be convicted of smuggling the vase.

As one looked around the room that day, the values and labels attached to the krater seemed to multiply. To journalists who asked officials about the insured value of the krater, the vase became an object of commerce that needed a price tag. To others, it was an artwork to be admired for its aesthetic qualities. To some of the reporters, the krater was at once an artwork and merchandise, or even other things, depending on how much they were concerned with the political and archaeological issues. In short, one pot in one room, entangled in a network of relationships, had what seemed to be endlessly different meanings to the dozens of people there. Yet what the guests in the room had in common was the thing itself, and their roles in its life story.

All eyes were on the stout outline of the vase, cloaked in its white sheet. "Now let's uncover what is hidden here, the Euphronios krater," the culture minister said, setting off an excited rumble in the crowd as guests readied their cameras and craned their necks. A white-coated archaeologist from the Culture Ministry, and a deliveryman in blue jeans who had brought the krater from the airport, stood on either side of the table and lifted the sheet. As cameras flashed, the room burst into cheers for the return of the krater to the land where it had been buried more than two millennia before.

When the so-called Euphronios Krater first surfaced at the Met in 1972, scholars knew of just three other pots that Euphronios had signed as a vase painter throughout his career in Athens during the 6th century B.C. By the end of February 1973, word had leaked out that yet another such rarity had appeared on the antiquities market, this one a kylix (cup for drinking wine). Amazingly, the kylix and the krater bore the same Trojan War scene, one seldom found on Greek vases: the death of Sarpedon, a Lycian prince and son of Zeus, who in Homer's epic defended Troy and died there because his anguished father chose not to abuse his godly powers to spare him.

The life stories of these two red-figure Attic vases by Euphronios aren't just compelling archaeological tales, but jumping-off points for tackling the problems of ownership and value-creation in the antiquities trade. Current debates over antiquities collecting and cultural property often overlook the stories of an object's ownership and identities in favor of the dominant question, "Where should they be?" Yet there are both practical and theoretical implications to tracing histories. The research that goes into compiling an object's biography can include archival work, interviews, and site studies that reveal new information, such as find spots of vases and life stories of influential dealers. Even if legal processes or negotiated settlements do sometimes resolve the "Where should they be?" question, an object biography can shed additional light on the forces that lie at the heart of the antiquities trade itself, and more broadly, on the dynamics of material culture. The example of the antiquities trade demonstrates how the metaphor of biography has become a tool to understand the relationship between things and humans, from the creation of the objects, to the introduction of the key human actors such as consumers and curators, to the combination of the two into networks where objects and people create value and meaning for each other over time.

The krater vase for mixing water and wine – known as a calyx krater for the way its upturned handles make it look like the inside (calyx) of a flower – stands 45.7 cm high. Its primary outer surface depicts Hypnos (Sleep) and Thanatos (Death) lifting the body of the fallen Sarpedon. Stripped of its armor, Sarpedon gushes blood as Sleep and Death carry out the wishes of his father that his body be spirited away for burial, in his homeland of Lycia in Asia Minor. The reverse side of the krater shows warriors donning battle gear. The names of Euphronios (as painter) and Euxitheos (as potter) are painted on the pot. Another inscription, *Leagros kalos* ("Leagros is beautiful"), refers to a known Athenian individual and places the krater's creation in the penultimate decade of the 6th century B.C.

The kylix, by contrast, is a short, stemmed wine-cup with a broad bowl from which to drink. It is 11.5 cm high, with a diameter of 33.0 cm at its rim – about the size of an LP record. Its primary outer surface depicts Sarpedon being carried from left to right by Thanatos, who heaves Sarpedon over his shoulder, and Hypnos, who lifts Sarpedon's legs. The other side of the cup depicts a warrior dancing, with a woman, a flute player, and a youth looking on. Euphronios' signature as the cup's painter is written on the edge of the kylix's foot.

The timeline of these two vases begins before their manufacture, going back thousands of years to the mythical Trojan War battle in which Sarpedon perished. In about 515 B.C., in Athens, the potter and painter Euphronios commemorated the death of Sarpedon by depicting it on both the kylix and krater, which were exported to Etruria in central Italy. Etruscans buried the vases as tomb offerings in the town of Caere, today known as the modern town of Cerveteri. The pots did not see the light of day again for some 2,400 years.

This moment of burial should not be seen as the end of a vase's biography, as much as its modern excavation should not be seen as its beginning. In his article "Notes on the Life History of a Pot Sherd," archaeologist Cornelius Holtorf uses a pottery fragment found at a dig in Sicily to examine the way objects' life histories are told, sometimes in short life histories (until burial) and sometimes in long ones that go through to the present. He writes that the life stories continue through excavation, analysis, exhibition and beyond. "A study of the life history of things must therefore not assume anything about *what they are*, but try to understand *how they come to be* ancient artefacts or whatever else," he writes (2002: 55). This is another way, in the context of the antiquities trade, of seeking answers to the question "Where have they been?"

To follow the ways in which the meanings of material get made in the present, we can turn to the human actors from the 20th century whose lives were to become entwined with the biographies of the Euphronios kylix and krater. Dietrich von Bothmer, schooled in Germany, went on to be appointed as the chairman of the Metropolitan Museum of Art's Greek and Roman Department. He had seen a vase by Euphronios in a Berlin museum and was inspired to follow his passion for Greek pots to Oxford, where he studied with the late Sir John Beazley. Robert Hecht, an heir to an American department store fortune, moved to Italy after World War II on a fellowship at the American Academy at Rome, but ended up becoming one of the world's most influential antiquities dealers. Most important among the human players whose lives would intersect the biographies of the Sarpedon krater and kylix was Giacomo Medici; he rose to be a conduit between the Italian antiquities underworld of tomb robbers and the foreign dealers, such as Hecht, who supply the West's great museums. Medici's father provided for his growing family by digging up artifacts in the necropolises around Rome and selling his finds at a stand in the Piazza Borghese market. Young Giacomo paid little attention to the trade until the family fled Rome during World War II to settle on land that was once ancient Etruria. An Italian prince who traced his family line back to the Greek hero Herakles, and who lived in a palace near the Medici's home, befriended Medici and showed him his private antiquities collection. He was entranced by the status that collecting brought to the prince and the connection to the past that it gave him, enhancing his noble origins. So, after graduating from a technical school with an electrician's diploma, Medici followed family tradition into the art trade in the 1960s.

At the same time, the two vases by Euphronios, buried for two and a half millennia, re-started their biographical journey. Medici's decade of peddling mediocre antiquities to Italian clients while building connections with tomb robbers paid off with one major find that catapulted him from Rome's outdoor markets into the international trade. Just before Christmas 1971, clandestine diggers opened a tomb in Cerveteri and pulled out at least one (the krater) of the two Euphronios pots depicting Sarpedon – an episode of looting that has been the subject of a number of books and popular articles since the early 1970s. The second vase, the kylix, also surfaced around the same time, possibly from the same tomb. Medici bought and then re-sold both vases down two very different paths.

One vase, the krater, set a record in 1972 for the highest price ever paid for an ancient artwork when the Metropolitan Museum of Art bought it for $1 million via American dealer Robert Hecht, first authenticating it through Oxford University's Research Laboratory for Archaeology and the History of Art with a thermoluminescence test to make sure it was genuinely ancient. The pot became a world-famous jewel of the Met's Greek and Roman collection: the Euphronios Krater.

The smaller cup, also decorated with the death of Sarpedon, took a less public journey. Medici sold the cup to Hecht for $25,000, but when Hecht tried to sell it to the Met in 1973 for $70,000, the museum's director, Thomas Hoving, refused, spooked by the bad publicity he attracted with the purchase of the Euphronios krater, which *The New York Times* and *Observer* of London had revealed may have come from illicit digging in Italy. Adding to the suspicion that the vase came from a recently robbed tomb, the Met curator von Bothmer disclosed that the Euphronios Krater has a smaller twin – the kylix. The unlikely coincidence was the first public hint that the kylix existed.

As a result, Hecht kept the kylix private, finally selling the cup in 1979, through his business partner Bruce McNall, owner of the L.A. Kings ice-hockey team, to the billionaire Bunker Hunt of Dallas for about $800,000. The kylix travelled to Los Angeles, where the J. Paul Getty Museum displayed and published the cup for the first time. Martin Robertson, who had been Oxford University's Lincoln Professor of Classical Archaeology – Beazley's old post – wrote an article on it for a Getty publication.

Hunt then sent the kylix and the rest of his collection on a year-long, four-museum, United States tour. The Met's von Bothmer was one of the contributors to the catalogue of that travelling exhibit, playing a role again in the biography of the kylix.

When Hunt went bankrupt trying to corner the silver bullion market, he sold the kylix for $742,500 at a 1990 Sotheby's auction in New York. The entry in the auction catalogue was acknowledged in its Preface to be an adaptation of that in the earlier catalogue for the travelling exhibition. The buyer was a "European Dealer" – none other than Giacomo Medici. Medici outbid the Met, in the person of von Bothmer, who said in a later interview that he considered the loss the low point of his career. Because Sotheby's kept Medici's identity secret, the cup's whereabouts became a puzzle. The kylix is the only Euphronios work listed in the Beazley Archive database with an "unknown" location.

At the same time, Medici had arrived at the pinnacle of the trade, opening a gallery in Geneva that sold the world's greatest museums and richest collectors artifacts dug up by a network of tomb robbers. He sold hundreds of illicitly excavated or exported artifacts (anonymously, but ultimately traceably) through Sotheby's in London, attracting investigators' attention. On Sept. 13, 1995, as he vacationed in Sardinia with his family, Swiss and Italian police raided Medici's warehouse in Geneva. The subsequent legal cases against him laid bare a trafficking network that led to America's biggest museums and best-known collectors. The 1995 Geneva raid was also a turning point for the Euphronios kylix decorated with Sarpedon. Police found the cup in a fireproof safe in the Geneva warehouse, but during a 1998 inventory a Swiss inspector dropped the kylix, which shattered into some 100 fragments. After photographing the sherds, the police swept them into plastic bags.

Over the next decade, Medici's world unravelled along with the entire global trade in antiquities. An Italian judge seized his Maserati automobile and his antiquities collection, comprising thousands of objects that were trucked from his Swiss warehouse to Italy, including the broken kylix, which was stored in a cardboard box at the Villa Giulia museum. Medici went on trial in Rome, where he was convicted in 2004 of smuggling, receiving stolen antiquities and conspiracy to traffic in stolen antiquities.

The evidence against Medici was enough to convince museum directors they should give back to Italy the antiquities for which he had been convicted. In 2006, the Met ended its three-decade dispute with Italy and finally agreed to return the Euphronios Krater. Without admitting wrongdoing, the Met conceded that the krater was discovered in Cerveteri, north of Rome, and was therefore the legal property of the Italian government. Italian prosecutors also started trials against Medici's alleged co-conspirators: Hecht, who had bought and sold the pair of vases by Euphronios, and Marion True, the antiquities curator at the Getty Museum. The Getty also agreed to give Italy objects cited in the court cases, leaving gaps in its own collection as it surrendered unique pieces.

For years, the smaller Euphronios kylix remained in fragments, in plastic bags inside a cardboard box at a storeroom of Rome's Villa Giulia museum, until it was quietly repaired and put on display. In January 2008, the Met returned the Sarpedon krater by Euphronios to Italy, starting a new chapter in the biographies of the vases and the people whose lives are touched by them.

One way of understanding the antiquities trade is to put aside the question of ownership and look at a mix of ideas about exchange, value, identity, and agency that come out of anthropology. We can tell the stories of objects and people of the antiquities trade by using a biographical approach set out in 1986 by Igor Kopytoff, an anthropology professor who helped pioneer the study of the social lives of things. We can also add the idea that biographies are not just timelines, but can be seen as networks in which actors become intertwined over time.

The biography of a thing can be explored like that of a person, Kopytoff wrote. "Where does the thing come from and who made it? What has been its career so far, and what do people consider to be an ideal career for such things?" (1986: 66). "To us, a biography of a painting by Renoir that ends up in an incinerator is as tragic, in its way, as the biography of a person who ends up murdered," he writes, adding that there are also more subtle events in an artwork's "life" such as whether it ends up in a private collection away from public view, or leaves France for the United States or, say, Nigeria. "The cultural responses to such biographical details reveal a tangled mass of aesthetic, historical and even political judgements, and of convictions and values that shape our attitudes to objects labelled 'art'" (1986: 67).

How can we best understand the tangled mass of these biographies? Networks, as conceptualised by the French philosopher Bruno Latour help provide a framework. He takes the human property of agency and applies it to the non-human, as it relates to other things and people. In the case of the Euphronios vases, the pots, curators, auction houses, museums, and prosecutors transform each other through their relations. Things, people (and hybrids of both) come together to form what Latour describes as "actor-networks." In such a system, the actor is "not the source of an action but the moving target of a vast array of entities swarming toward it" (2005: 46).

Latour's actor-networks tie together the story-telling of object biography with the rich lessons drawn from the ethnography of the circulation of things in Melanesia, long studied for the ways in which islanders exchange shell arm-bands and other goods laden with ritual, social, and entrepreneurial meanings. These exchanges in which ownership histories become attached to objects, whether they involve beads, canoes, or pigs, comprise networks that are similar in ways to those described by Latour. The exchange goods can have agency, and can be seen as actors in social networks of people and things. Anthropologist Marilyn Strathern, looking specifically at the ways people and things interact in this Melanesian context, even turned these networks inside-out by arguing in 1988 that people themselves are the objectifications of relationships. Her concept of "relational personhood" combines two important ideas: that things circulate as parts of persons, which is classic Melanesian anthropology of the gift, and the additional idea that people themselves are capable of circulating through the things with which they have contact.

If people and things can be seen as having life histories as actors in networks that are grounded in social relations, then, with the help of object biography as a tool for exposing those connections, we can start to imagine how a web of relations came together around the Euphronios vases. And a picture emerges that supports the argument for extending personhood to things. The 2008 return to Italy of the Euphronios krater in Rome – in which it was welcomed in a ceremony by dozens of people whose lives had been affected by the pot – demonstrated how an object itself had become imbued with the distributed personhood of the people it had touched.

The role of a person as an actor may be more intuitive than that of an object-as-actor, but in this case it is important to see how these human actors fit into a network in which they share their actor roles with the things. By including these objects as actors in a network, we can tell more complete stories of vases (and their people) through their life histories. Excluding the agency of these objects would leave gaps in understanding both people and things.

Of course, we're tracing the life histories of these vases because they ended up being bought and sold. Curators and collectors lusted after them; writers wanted to discover their secrets. In short, they were valuable – in many different ways. How value is built up, especially through prestige, is crucial to understanding the contemporary antiquities trade. Ideas of prestige are engrained in the practice of archaeology, particularly in relation to grave goods that archaeologists associate with being indicators of a person's status in the distant and not-so-distant past. In prehistory, archaeologists have used the emergence of prestige goods as a marker of the transition from unspecialised economic systems to large-scale exchange-based economies, and the presence of rich goods as reflective of high status. But it might just be that rich goods themselves, such as gold objects, have created high status in people– a point that has resonance in the practices of the contemporary antiquities trade. When it comes to the possession of "rich objects," archaeologist Colin Renfrew wrote, "By virtue of the prestige it confers, ownership offers access to social networks and to other resources that are closed to those lacking such prestige" (1986: 161). In the antiquities trade, owners and possessors help write an object's biography and give it value (financial and otherwise), while objects do exactly the same thing for their owners and possessors, conferring prestige. How both people and objects accrue prestige and other meanings through the biographical arc can explain a key process in biography, both as theory and when applied to the antiquities trade.

The ability of an object to define a person's self can expand to include groups of objects in museums or collections of antiquities. In the cases of Giacomo Medici the merchant, Dietrich von Bothmer the curator, or Bunker Hunt the collector, the process of accumulating or being associated with objects helped create their biographies. These men, and others like them, came to define themselves through the groups of objects they handled and the prestige they gained from doing so. They sought new objects – such as the Sarpedon kylix by Euphronios that was a match to the Sarpedon krater at the Met – because they complemented other objects that had already helped define who they were as people.

While the process of objects and people influencing each other's biographies is mutual, some of these actors have more power than their counterparts. In the antiquities trade, certain people and institutions possess outsized power, and frequently can change or define the biographies of objects. Such processes are particularly of interest where clandestinely dug artifacts of undocumented origin can gain new biographies, and a sheen of legitimacy, from display in museums or via academic publication and authentication. People associated with these institutions and the related objects, moreover, can gain prestige.

Prestige and authenticity are just examples of the many types of values at play in the antiquities trade (and, indeed, in archaeology). What we see emerging from the multiple types of contacts between humans and objects over time is the creation of value. These values accrue and change as people and events define ancient artworks (such as the Euphronios vases) and the people and other objects with which they are entwined. Publishing, exhibiting, and academic authentication, lead to various other types of value – financial, artistic, historic, fame, pleasure, professional advancement, celebrity, and prestige.

This discussion of value brings us full circle back to object biographies. The Sarpedon krater gained part of its prestige and fame, because the Metropolitan Museum paid $1 million for it. The price was a record at the time, and the vase became known as "the million-dollar pot." The high monetary value of such works has the ability to confer a series of non-financial values. There's nothing like a big price tag to transform an artwork into a "priceless museum masterpiece." And the people associated with big-ticket items, such as curators and collectors, also accrue new importance. In turn, these people can turn their own prestige values back into money; their reputations as rich collectors win them seats on boards of trustees of museums, which in turn stage exhibits of objects they own, which gain in financial value as a result. As a benefit of their social-collector prestige, the American owners can donate these objects to American museums, earning a tax credit in the process.

But what is crucial to understanding the antiquities trade is how the value of prestige – when entwined with issues of ownership and the life histories of people and things – opens windows onto motivations, forces, and networks that drive that trade and can provide insights into ending the abuses by people and institutions who seek that prestige.

Financial value is one of just many types of values that people can attach to archaeological material. To be sure, there are the artistic, scientific, sacred, or practical values of an artifact, yet the market view is the one that is most closely associated with the destructive forces of the antiquities trade. But how is that value generated? To find out, I dug through eight years of Sotheby's antiquities auction results – entering each price into a spreadsheet, along with the prices the auction house expected to make – and cross-referenced each of the thousands of entries with information about the object that had been contained in the catalogs. It turned out that the financial value was closely linked with all those other types of non-financial values, such as whether they'd passed through the hands of prestige-granting people and institutions such as museums, universities, and academics. Who handled things, published them, authenticated them, and what is known about their archaeological origins, all play a significant role in determining market value.

Using the online Sotheby's auction results, I examined 18 antiquities auctions in New York from December 2000 through December 2008, combining their history and archaeology categories into one "provenance" that ranks the earliest known date of an object's existence, and adding several other categories to show whether the objects had been anointed in some way by a prestige-granting institution or person.

In all, I evaluated 2,616 auction lots for the following types of "provenance" as listed in the Sotheby's catalogues: predating 1971 (the cut-off for the UNESCO convention that protects cultural heritage); postdating 1970; a provenance with no specific date; and no provenance given at all. I also sorted them by which had been exhibited, published, or authenticated by an academic or a university, or had some connection to a museum, including ownership by a curator. The survey also tracked the auction house's estimated price range for each lot and then took an average of the high and low estimate, which was compared with the actual sale price at auction.

Those that had stamps of approval from experts or institutions (at least one instance of being published, exhibited, having a museum connection, or academic authentication) sold for 132 percent higher than the estimate, versus those that had no such imprimatur, which sold for 81 percent higher than the estimate. The lots with a listed history predating 1971 sold for 135 percent above the average estimate, while those lacking such an early known history sold for 71 percent above the auction estimate. That means the length of an artifact's known modern biography and whether it preceded the UNESCO convention appeared to have a strong influence on how much people were willing to pay. Taken together, provenance date and prestige pack the biggest punch in the auction hall. Lots with histories listed before 1971 *and* any of the prestige imprimaturs sold for 156 percent above the auction estimate, while those lacking both had a below-average premium of 69 percent.

Overall, the numbers show that antiquities with long, documented histories, and connections to museums, professors, and publishers, exceed their estimated auction prices by a greater margin than objects that lack these qualities. The auction data of these thousands of items only gives a hint of the forces at work in an object's biography. But money isn't everything.

On the final day of the Sarpedon krater's exhibition in New York, visitors to the Metropolitan Museum of Art read passages from the *Iliad* aloud in the vase's presence – almost as incantations. At the unveiling in Rome, the culture minister did the same, reading Homer as the white sheet came off the pot, invoking mythical events predating the creation of the object itself. This, too, is important. If the network in which the two Euphronios vases are enmeshed is allowed to include myth, it expands beyond time and space into the world of hybrid beings such as monsters and deities. In the end, the life stories of two very real vases by Euphronios blur the lines between the material and the mythological. The powers of objects, whether derived through their style, technology, or the stories in their decoration, make them actors in networks that have implications for archaeology and understanding the past, ones that extend far beyond legal or moral ownership in the present.

The Decline and Fall of the Classic Maya City

Keith Eppich

…The vicissitudes of fortune, which spares neither man nor the proudest of his works, which buries empires and cities in a common grave…

Edward Gibbon, *The Decline and Fall of the Roman Empire* (1776–89), Ch. 71.

A buried residence at El Perú-*Waka'* with the underbrush cleared away.
(Photo by Keith Eppich.)

As strange as it sounds, the dead Maya cities tend to sneak up on you. These urban ruins lie underneath a thousand years of tropical growth, covered by the voracious plant life of a living rainforest. One walks down jungle paths surrounded by the myriad sights, sounds, and smells of the Central American jungle. There are chirping birds, buzzing insects, and the sudden rustle of larger animals moving through underbrush. Spider monkeys gaze down from the high forest branches, interested in this strange primate walking across the forest floor, wondering perhaps why anyone would do something so foolish. There are big cats in these woods, jaguars and pumas, not to mention a variety of vicious and venomous snakes. At midday, sunlight streams through the dense tree canopies, dappling the forest floor in shadow and light. In the areas of heavy forest, the sunlight can vanish entirely and a viewer is left in the heavy midday dark of towering trees. As the light dims, the forest floor grows quieter and, if you're alone, the air seems to gain weight. At times, it can be spooky, even on well-traveled paths.

Off to the sides of the path, you start to see lumps and mounds on the forest floor, mixed in with the speckled light and undergrowth. The first few times you see them, they're nothing special, just another piece of crumpled ground in an uneven terrain. All this landscape formed on a limestone bedrock and the uneven, broken ground that comes with such bedrock. After a dozen such sightings, the mounds begin to look familiar. There's a pile of rubble scattered here or there, with a slender tree perched on top, bending over the leaf-covered mound. Then the heaps seem to arrange themselves into patterns: they form rough rectangles or conical shapes in and among the trees. It dawns on you that these things are buildings – or all that remains of buildings abandoned to the forest for a millennium. At this point, it's hard not to stop and stare. Once you make out one building, you make out a second, a third, then ten more in quick succession. The entirety of the dead city unfolds around you, almost at once. You're not just walking along a jungle path: you're walking through the middle of a Classic Maya city.

Part of this has to do with Central American rainforests, being paradoxically strong and fragile at the same time. In contrast to the more familiar forests of the temperate north, rainforests possess dozens of tree species mixed together. Unlike a pine or oak-birch forest, the tropical forests mix towering ramons, spike-barked ceibas, dark cedars, black mahoganies, white-flowered sapodillas, and red gumbo-limbo trees with their distinctive thin, peeling bark. The number of plant species in a single square kilometer easily crosses into the triple digits. Each takes advantage of its own precise requirements for water, soil, and sunlight. The soil of the forest floor is infamously poor, the majority of the nutrients being locked into the mass of vegetation above. This biodiversity allows quick recovery of small cleared patches, the hundreds of species rapidly colonizing new areas. Trees live and die, and their rotting remains nourish successive generations of plant life. Many of the old Maya cities lie beneath centuries of this cycle of growth, death, and rebirth. Once large areas of the forest are clear-cut, however, the soil rapidly decays; thin soils wash away, leaving only a sun-baked laterite, a dense, hardpan soil heavy with metals, largely incapable of supporting plant life. Large sections of the limestone bedrock are visible in clear-cut and over-farmed portions of Guatemala today. This high biodiversity, once removed from large areas, returns only with great difficulty and considerable time. In these forests small wounds heal quickly, but deep ones are fatal.

But then there's the matter of how the Classic Maya built their cities. For the most part, and for much of their history, Maya cities lacked city gates, high fortified walls, or indeed apparent boundaries of any kind. There was no distinction between urban and rural, between town and country. Beginning with a built-up core of pyramids, palaces, and plazas, Maya settlements faded out in slow gradation to open, uninhabited forests. Often the distant hinterland of one city would overlap with the distant hinterland of its neighbor. The Classic Maya had no centralized planning and just watched their cities grow where they lay, with extensive suburbs and small communities lying in the urban periphery. One might say that the cities resembled the forests in which they lived, each human settlement taking advantage of local conditions of water, soil, and sunlight. Like the rainforest itself, the Maya cities had their own cycles of growth, death, and rebirth. Hence the dead cities sprawl across the forest floor, with buildings occurring in uneven clumps that increase closer to the old urban cores, the structures half-hidden by both the verdant forest and their own ruination.

The city of El Perú-*Waka'* is no exception to this pattern. Its ruined center lies in the heart of the Laguna del Tigre National Park in northwestern Guatemala, and reaching it requires a full day of travel – that is, if everything goes as planned. My fellow archaeologists and I usually begin the day in the Zona Central, the modern towns clustered around the central lakes of the Petén, the northernmost province of Guatemala. The three main towns, San Benito, Santa Elena, and the island-town of Flores form the urban core of the Zona Central on the southern shore of Lago Petén Itzá. These are little towns whose residents love poured concrete. They have concrete masonry buildings, poured concrete roads, paved concrete sidewalks, and molded cement water fountains. This turns the towns into hot, dry constructions, from whose streets the tropical sun reflects in a merciless torrent. In the modern Guatemalan Zona Central, where many Maya people of the 21st century dwell, there are few trees and only little plants; the atmosphere tends to be hot and oppressive, redolent of gasoline and cooking oil. The people are bustling, propelling themselves into the future with great enthusiasm. There are hardware stores, tire depots, seed stores, dress shops, and many bars and restaurants. It is a type of urban development that could not be replicated across the rest of northern Guatemala without completely obliterating the tropical rainforest. Its spread has fueled deforestation across the region: much rainforest has already been destroyed, and the rest remains threatened.

This deforestation becomes apparent on the journey to El Perú-*Waka'*. Outside San Benito, the paved roads rapidly turn into hard-packed white limestone and our pick-up trucks kick up huge clouds of dust in their wake. The drivers are friendly, knowledgeable, and tend to drive as if possessed. Each village has irregular lines of limestone rocks jutting from the road-bed, improvised speedbumps. Even so, speeds are rarely moderated, and the local chickens, fat pigs, scrawny dogs, and small children seem to have acquired a special awareness of rapidly approaching traffic. I've never seen so much as a chicken disappear beneath someone's wheels, although I've heard many stories about them; little crosses on the roadside suggest that it is not only chickens that are crushed by passing cars. Cornfields cover the broken karstic hills and small valleys. Local farmers ride their horses along the roads, keeping a wary eye on traffic. The occasional tree on a hillside, standing forlornly in a cornfield, hints that this was not always the case. These are the lands cut from the forest, the corn sucking up the remaining nutrients from poor tropical soils. Most farms produce corn irregularly and many farmers hover on the edge of insolvency.

As we approach the edge of the surviving trees, the landscape changes. Here are the recently cut areas. The terrain ceases to look like a settled agrarian landscape and begins to resemble old photographs from Flanders in the First World War. The ground is blackened and torn, with tangles of barbed wire indicating the limits of old fields; broken and toppled trees, stubbornly resistant to flame, jut out from the earth. This is the forest cleared by machete and chainsaw and fire, prepared for planting. It's the edge of the environmental catastrophe slowly spreading across the last rainforests of northern Guatemala. A glance at a map gives even more cause for alarm: these recently slashed-and-burned fields are inside the bounds of the National Park. The streams and gullies of the area are thick with silt, topsoil washing away with each falling drop of rain. There is a lot of rain in the tropics.

Before crossing into the jungle proper, our little caravan of trucks stops at the village of Paso Caballos, near the headwaters of the Río San Pedro Mártir. The local Q'eqchi Maya migrated from the highlands about 20 years ago and cut their village into the side of the Laguna del Tigre National Park. They maintain an uneasy relationship with the central government: after all, their village is inside the park limits and illegal. They regularly cut into the forest to plant beans, corn, squash, and chiles, and they hunt the local deer and wild turkeys. Yet they are carefully monitored by Guatemalan police and the National Army. The government has decided that the village can stay for now – at any rate, the political cost in moving the village would be high, as video of Guatemalan soldiers manhandling Maya women and children would conjure up unpleasant memories of the military genocides in the 1980s. So, for the meantime, a balance has been reached. As long as Paso Caballos stays about the same size and doesn't cut too many trees, Guatemalan authorities seem content to leave them be. The problem is that after 10 years of working in and around Paso Caballos, we've seen the village growing, and the cuts in the forest seem deeper every year. If one types "Paso Caballos, Guatemala" into Google Earth, the resulting image is a small village surrounded by square patches of light and dark green: the dark green is tropical rainforest, light green cleared cornfield. There is a lot of light green. Paso Caballos is not static; each year the modern Maya cut deeper into the forest.

Into this unsettled situation stepped the Proyecto Arqueológico El Perú-*Waka'*. Founded by David Freidel and Hector Escobedo in 2003, it has grown into a multi-institutional research project examining the ruins of the ancient city and assisting other projects in the study and documentation of the rainforest. Both village and government have welcomed the archaeologists: government officials value our assistance in preserving the forest, while the locals see us as a way to cement their foothold in the park. Yet this relationship has waxed and waned over time. One year, for example, one of our trucks simply vanished. We left it parked next to the riverbank and, in the middle of a crowded village where everyone knows everyone, it disappeared. No one saw or heard a thing. We do hire a number of locals from the village to help with the excavations and train them as guides for the eco-tourists who come through from time to time. For the most part, the Q'eqchi from Paso are polite, hard-working men who seem to have become quite attached to "their ruins." They view the ruins as their own and are rather proprietary and protective of the tumbled remains. Looting at the old city has decreased significantly since 2003 and, when looters tried to break into a major tomb at the site core, the local Q'eqchi were as angry as the archaeologists.

Once past Paso Caballos and a few of its outlying farms, we enter the real jungle. It's a heavy, multi-canopied rainforest, thick with growth. The trees grasp the soil with outstretched roots and the undergrowth clusters around and among the trunks. The road becomes decidedly uneven and the trucks tend to sway and buckle. The road is little more than a thin path among, between, and below the great trees. If a car is going to break, it's going to do so along the jungle road between Paso Caballos and the ruins of El Perú-Waka'. Winches become a necessity in the rainy season and the tilting path has been known to snap an axle or two. The track itself winds between a high escarpment on the north and the river to the south; it begins to climb slightly.

This escarpment is the reason the Classic Maya built the old city where they did. It is a natural upthrust of limestone, forming a roughly triangular tabletop that towers a good 80 m above the surrounding terrain. To the south and west of it are the rivers and extensive swampy wetlands. To the north and east, the escarpment breaks up into a series of broken hills and defiles. The tabletop itself, however, is roughly even and well-drained, a natural and commanding redoubt. The city sprawls across this tabletop, with settlements scattered along the river, at the edge of the wetlands, and across the broken hills.

This much is apparent as the trucks buck and steer their way along the jungle road. Off to the sides, among the trees, small mounds and rectangular piles of debris mark where these outlying communities once stood. Even with a practiced eye, distinguishing between a ruin and a natural feature is difficult, but the strange lumps and mounds under the trees occur more frequently as the line of trucks nears the base camp. Picking out ruined houses gets easier as the mounds and scatters of debris become more common. And so do the animals of the rainforest – spider monkeys, wild turkeys, the big American rodents, *sereques* and *tepezcuintles*. The forest's most famous inhabitants are the jaguars, after whom the Laguna del Tigre is named. A 2005 study of the jaguars in the park revealed a number of active cats, including one large 80-kg male. It's environmentally encouraging, although not personally reassuring, to have so many big cats. Jaguars will hunt people, and we are encouraged not to wander the forest at night. Second to the jaguars are the scarlet macaws, the *guacamayas*. These large and spectacularly-plumed birds mate for life and call to each other with harsh, primordial shrieks. They like to inhabit the highest trees, preferring those already growing on the tops of ruined pyramids and palaces. While working at these structures, it's not uncommon to have macaws slowly circling the excavations, screeching at one another. They are highly prized and, in addition to looting the ruins, criminals often raid macaw nests, stealing chicks for the exotic pet market. In a 2004 shoot-out with park police, poachers were caught with a pair of young macaw chicks; the authorities arrested two poachers, but the stolen chicks did not survive the encounter. And then there are Morelet's Crocodiles, which can reach upwards of 3 m in length. The wetlands to the west of the site contain the largest number of crocodiles yet known in North America. Next to the waterways and lakes, park officials have placed large signs. "No Nadar," they say – "No swimming".

All of these animals would be endangered if the park collapses. Outside interests would very much like to log the park and replace forests with debtor farmers and ranchlands. The forests to the east have long since fallen: they're denuded of trees, jaguars, macaws, and crocodiles. A secondary goal of the Proyecto Arqueológico has been to maintain a public presence in the forest, to prevent illegal clearing and logging and looting and, thus far, our efforts have been successful: conservationists have privately confided in us that, if not for the archaeological project, large portions of that park would have been cleared. Research into the ancient Maya past can hold the modern rainforest together. That is especially ironic, given what we've uncovered about the end of Classic civilization.

The site core of El Perú-*Waka'* consists of dozens of sprawling palaces and towering pyramids arranged around a massive, rectangular Central Concourse, 280 m long and 80 m wide – larger than two football fields placed end-to-end, or about four baseball diamonds. On the northwest corner of the Concourse is the royal palace, while the southeast corner houses Structure M13-1, probably the main city temple; behind it lies the Chok Group, the second largest palace at the site and the former home of the royal cadet lineage. Tucked away between these sprawling palace-compounds are the more modest residences of the ancient city-dwellers. A ring of such smaller house compounds circles the urban core and trickles away as the habitations expand across and beyond the tabletop of the escarpment. An entire ritual complex with two massive pyramids stands on the far southeastern corner of the urban core, at the very edge of the escarpment. Standing on top of these pyramids, one looks straight down a 150 m drop to the river below. It's a dizzying view. In antiquity, these two great pyramids would have been visible from 20 or 30 km away, and no one passing on the river below could possibly have missed them: they were material symbols of authority and command. Research over the past 12 years has begun to reveal the size, shape, and history of this ancient city. What follows is a rough outline of what we know so far.

El Perú-*Waka'* was one of 40-odd city-states of the Classic Maya, who inhabited the southern third of Mexico, the northern portions of El Salvador and Honduras, and all of modern-day Guatemala and Belize. Beginning in the first few centuries A.D., their cities rose from the ruins of previous civilizations and spread across the broad tropical lowlands. The heart of classic Maya culture lay in the big urban centers clustered in northern Guatemala, an area known as the Petén. Sheltered here, a remarkable civilization flourished. Maya astronomers tracked the movement of cosmic bodies from atop towering pyramids; they named the constellations and predicted the waxing and waning of the traveling planets. They developed sophisticated mathematical knowledge, with both notational placement and the concept of zero. They built pyramids with regular right angles that require a close familiarity with geometry. Their sophisticated script, the famous Maya hieroglyphs, recorded a great deal of astronomical data and tracked the movement of cosmic bodies in the sky. They blended art and history onto large-scale monuments laden with carved texts. These texts largely consist of rituals and genealogies of ruling kings and queens, births, accessions, wars, deaths, and ceremonies to mark the passage of holy time. We know they also possessed folding bark-paper books, as such books appear in Maya art. To date, no such Classic text has ever been recovered. Of hundreds of such books possessed in the 16th century, only four survived the brutality of the Spanish Conquest.

An elegant culture thrived in the Classic cities, one that had markets and merchants, currency and literacy. From our perspective, ceramic arts excelled all others, and beautiful, fragile Maya vessels have made their way to famous museums. Indeed, the looters who tear through these ancient cities today do so in hope of finding such vessels intact. A single piece of looted Maya ceramic art can result in tens of thousands of dollars of ill-gotten gain.

The cities themselves, however, may well be the most remarkable achievement of the Classic Maya. They were large and held massive populations, perhaps in excess of 100,000 in the case of the biggest Maya city-states, according to some researchers. This makes Maya urban conglomerations roughly comparable with those of Classical Greece, including Athens herself. But unlike the cities of Plato and Thucydides, those of the Maya were built in the forbidding environment of the tropical rainforest. The largest modern towns of the Zona Central possess only about half this number of residents, and have deforested large swaths of their surroundings. By contrast, the classic Maya cities not only lay in the rainforest, but flourished there for centuries. For most of their occupation they were ecologically sustainable in a manner that modern cities are not.

The historical sequence for El Perú-*Waka'* seems fairly typical for a Classic Maya city. Originally, it was a series of farmsteads scattered across that tabletop escarpment. Around A.D. 100 or so, these farmsteads coalesced into a small town located on the escarpment's western edge. The town formed the center of the dense urban core that was to follow. In about the fourth century, the ancient Maya built the Central Concourse, laid the foundations of the palaces and pyramids, raised monumental art, and inscribed it with their history. Outside of the site core, farms and outlying settlements spread across and around the escarpment. While not the largest of the Classic Maya cities, El Perú-*Waka'* rapidly evolved into one of the most important of the Classic kingdoms, since it sat astride two of the most vital trade routes of the era. The kings of El Perú-*Waka'* held influence far greater than the size of their city would suggest: the most powerful of the Maya cities regularly entreated the kings of El Perú-*Waka'*, sending their daughters to be royal wives and mothers. The city was deeply involved in all the major events of Classic Maya history, from the dealings with the distant empire of Teotihuacan to the tangled alliances between cities of the fifth to eighth centuries. Hieroglyphic texts from that period tell of the city-states coming together into massive military alliances involving dozens of cities. The biggest Maya cities, Calakmul on one side and Tikal on the other, led these coalitions in military clashes throughout the seventh and eighth centuries.It seems to have been a seesaw of escalating wars that dragged on from A.D. 560 to 800, with city-states switching sides, making and breaking agreements, even launching wars on their own brothers. The unlucky cities burned. And in the eighth century, Classic Maya civilization came apart at the seams in what scholars refer to simply as "The Collapse." The Collapse remains a series of poorly understood events that lasted from 750 to about 950, culminating in the abandonment of all the big Maya cities and almost all the smaller ones as well. Classic civilization ceased to exist throughout the Maya Lowlands and the rainforest we know today grew over the dead cities, cloaking them from view.

The main research goals at El Perú-*Waka'* were originally twofold. One was to explore the concepts of Classic Maya urbanism, to try and understand urban sustainability in the middle of a fragile ecosystem. The other was to investigate the nature of the Maya Collapse, as expressed at El Perú-*Waka'*. While the Collapse unfolded across the Classic world, El Perú-*Waka'* outlasted most of its fellows. Most Maya cites perished in one way or another in the eighth and ninth centuries, but El Perú-*Waka'* lingered on until the tenth century, being one of the last of the old cities to fall, dying around

A.D. 1000. So it can provide a unique perspective on whatever happened during this period. What we didn't expect was for these two goals to merge.

First, the Classic cities do not look like cities are supposed to look – or rather, they do not resemble the traditional urban pattern of Europe and North America. They are dispersed across the landscape, with a built-up urban core that peters out into the forest. While most team members were drawn to excavations within this core, Damien Marken explored the whole of the ancient urban pattern. He's been out in the peripheries, mapping and excavating distant residences and tracking their habitation through time. What he's found has been fascinating. The cityscape of El Perú-*Waka'* was dotted with neighborhood clusters mixed together with cultivated fields, garden plots, small forests, artificial lakes, swampy lowlands, and small streams – a mix we can term *low-density urbanism*. Instead of a clearly delineated city, it's almost easier to imagine it as an "urbanized countryside" centered roughly on an urban core. The rulers and powerful noble families dwelt within this core, which also held a central market as well as pyramids and temples. But most of the population lived, and virtually all the farming took place, in the highly scattered hinterland, held together by the political and ritual power of the city center. A Maya city would probably have resembled a patchwork quilt: farms, fields, gardens, roads, forests, wetlands, and lakes, all mixed together with homes and neighborhoods.

The strangeness of Classic cities fueled considerable debate in the 1990s. They differed so radically from the traditional idea of "city" that some scholars argued that they were not cities at all, that there was no Classic Maya urban tradition. This debate came to an end in the 2000s with the publication of extremely detailed maps of some of these Maya cities, showing the density and structure of Classic settlement. Human history, moreover, shows that there exists more than a single type of city. If the Classic cities of the Maya world do not resemble Athens and Rome, they do look like cities elsewhere, especially in Southeast Asia: Angkor Wat is an excellent example of a great metropolis built on a pattern of low-density urbanism. No one would deny that Angkor Wat is a "true city."

The unintentional purpose of the low-density spread was probably ecological sustainability. Scattered across a broad area, the city did not press heavily on the tropical environment for resources. Standing forest was maintained throughout the center of the settlement, likely in winding green spaces threaded throughout the low-density city. Cornfields left to fallow would rapidly return to forest. The urban blight of abandoned "dead zones," characteristic of any city, would be undone, as the tropical rainforest quickly closes over small gaps in the standing tree cover. For good reason, scholars have termed such settlements "green cities" or "garden cities." The scattered neighborhoods and farmsteads would have taken advantage of local conditions of sunlight, soil, and water. The human city in the Classic Maya past mirrored the rainforest itself, being highly diverse, highly scattered, highly sustainable. But then something happened.

Our second research goal consisted of understanding the series of events collectively known as "the Maya Collapse" that began to unfold by the mid-eighth century. From around A.D. 750 or so, the Maya cities began to fall apart, one by one. Preceded by a surge of population, Tikal crumbled around 850; its great rival to the north, the major city of Calakmul, only slightly outlived it, losing three-quarters of its population between 850 and 900; and the rest of the Maya world disintegrated in patches. The western Petén seems to have been hit particularly hard, with many of its cities experiencing violent, permanent ends in fire and death. Other cities prospered amid the chaos, likely housing refugee populations, but this only delayed the end, and they in turn dissolved by A.D. 1000. Still other areas weathered the storm, including some in the Zona Central itself. Populations declined, but eventually found their lower limit. In the east, particularly in the river valleys of Belize, the countryside seemed little touched by the chaos to the west: there, some small cities continued through the collapse, surviving even to witness the arrival of the Spanish five centuries later. It's a patchy, uneven event, what Arthur Demarest has termed a "nested series of collapses." The overall impression is a landscape in great tumult.

Still, no one really knows what happened. At one time, scholars argued that the Maya vanished under a catastrophic earthquake; a large-scale peasant revolt was once envisioned, as were widespread crop failure, epidemic disease, foreign invasion, and even some kind of New Age ascension into pure energy. All seem equally unlikely. More recently, "Maya megadroughts" have been proposed, century-long droughts that left the countryside barren and empty. This too seems to have been debunked by Gyles Iannone's 2014 book, *The Great Maya Droughts in Cultural Context*. The floral and faunal data show little sign of apocalyptic drought, yet soil erosion and lowered rainfall do appear, paradoxically, in some of the area's geological history. Endemic warfare remains the best explanation, although not a perfect one. Certainly, in the eighth century, military alliances grew larger and more aggressive than in earlier periods. Hostile episodes are mentioned more often in the history recorded on stone monuments, and war imagery becomes more common. But could warfare alone bring down an entire civilization?

With such theories in mind, we turned to the ruins of El Perú-*Waka'*. Back in 2003, when we first began digging in the center of the old city, we discovered thousands of sherds from the ninth and tenth centuries. These included big potsherds with thick, bolstered rims, finely carved orange serving vessels, and bowls with spider-monkey designs. Within the first month of excavation,

thousands of these late sherds turned into tens of thousands. El Perú-*Waka'*
was evidently one of the long-lived cities that survived the early stages of
collapse, making up one of those patches that apparently prospered as the rest
of the Classic Petén disintegrated. This ninth- and tenth-century occupation
was dense as well, every household and palace apparently full of inhabitants.
Each of those ruined houses, now slumbering beneath the forest floor, could
have held two or three families apiece. It must have been a very crowded city.

In early publications on El Perú-*Waka'*, we wrote with confidence that
this period, the 800s and 900s A.D., must have seen the city's population at
its height. But this turned out to be wrong – and Damien Marken showed
us why. Out wandering the hinterland to chart the urban settlement and
map the scattered neighborhoods, he found a very different pattern. He
encountered significant settlement throughout the area for the whole of the
Classic period, with the seventh and eighth centuries well-represented. El
Perú-*Waka'* had maintained prosperous, sustainable, low-density urbanism
that worked, and worked well. But that time came to an end. The decline
and fall of El Perú-*Waka'* began somewhere in the middle of the eighth
century. Across the urban hinterland, these far-flung neighborhoods and
scattered farmsteads drifted into ruin, and were almost wholly abandoned
by A.D. 800. While a few bitter-enders clung on in the periphery, for the
most part this scattered urbanism vanished, precisely as the population at
the core surged. Taking all the evidence together, the picture of the city's
decline becomes clear. The Maya of El Perú-*Waka'* flowed inward; they
fled the scattered farmsteads and distant neighborhoods of the river plains
and the broken hills; they flooded into the urban core on the tabletop
escarpment and retreated into the defensible heart of the city-state. This is not
a pattern unknown elsewhere in the Classic Maya world. Writing about the
archaeology of the southern Petén, Matt O'Mansky has eloquently described
how the collapse uncoiled. Only 120 km south of El Perú-*Waka'*, cities were
desperately fortified, then sacked and burned. The sole consideration for
settlement in the eighth century, he argues, was defensibility.

There exists a wonderful Italian word for this type of thing: *incastellamento*.
Translated into English, it becomes "encastlement." The term was coined by
a French scholar, Pierre Toubert (1973), to describe the mass construction
of fortified villages across medieval Europe. Beginning in the eighth century
A.D., as the nominal authority of post-Roman Europe disintegrated, those
living in the countryside realized that they were on their own in an angry
world. The solution lay in walls that were tall and thick. Cultivation was
limited to those areas in the immediate vicinity of those walls. Beyond that
was pasture for sheep and goats, wealth on the hoof that could be moved to
safety when Saracens or Germans threatened.

What we seem to have discovered, in the eighth and ninth century, is the *incastellamento* of the Maya world. The Maya abandoned the scattered cultivation of the countryside and crowded together in protected areas. In the case of El Perú-*Waka'*, this was the center of that natural tabletop escarpment, where they produced all the dense material culture we had first discovered in 2003. This "encastlement" marked the end of the low-density urbanism that had worked so well for centuries. New political and military considerations rendered low-density settlement obsolete. In urban studies across the world, numerous scholars have shown that nothing concentrates people faster and more effectively than war and political turmoil. The pattern of low-density urbanism was replaced by a concentrated high-density urbanism behind fortifications.

But this development brought its own problems. This is our current thinking about the end of El Perú-*Waka'*. A concentrated population, limited to the resources in the immediate vicinity of the city's core, would rapidly deplete those resources. Nearby forest would be cleared, and not by small cuts, easily healed from nearby stands of jungle, but by highly localized clear-cutting, as brutal as the modern deforestation of northern Guatemala. With the end of the local forest would come all the well-known problems of tropical deforestation, including significant depletion and erosion of soils. This turns forest topsoil into laterite, a landscape of which creates localized albedo effects that raise local temperature and lower local rainfall. For all intents and purposes, that hardpan might as well be poured concrete. Within a few decades, this high-density city would occupy the center of a man-made desert surrounded by tropical rainforest.

In short, the political and military situation of the eighth century seems to have dictated the development of a settlement pattern grotesquely out of alignment with the local environment. The sustainable low-density urbanism of previous centuries failed in the face of endemic warfare. The Maya sought security in high-density clusters, protected by their numbers and defenses, and, for a time, this new urban pattern worked. But high-density urbanism in a Maya rainforest is not sustainable; decline becomes inevitable, and one by one, these newly aligned cities perished. They didn't perish immediately, nor all at the same time, but their inevitable decline and fall created the patchy disintegration of the Classic Maya world. This led us to an insight about what seems to have happened in the eighth and ninth centuries. And it also married our two research goals.

From our current perspective, the Classic Maya Collapse was an urban collapse. It was the end of the forest cities of the Maya and the wondrous urban culture that flourished in them. It seems to explain the patchy and unsettled nature of the Classic collapse. Highly urbanized areas, the western and central Petén, were hit hardest, while less urbanized areas in the east and the river valleys of Belize were lightly touched and, in places, unaffected. It seems to explain why some cities show evidence of drought and erosion in the middle of an apparently healthy rainforest. It seems to explain why some places prospered amid the tumult, absorbing the refugees and wealth from dying cities, only to have their own resources slowly consumed. It seems to explain why the Post-Classic Maya lived in small villages, widely distributed across the forest. It seems to explain why El Perú-*Waka'*, with its broad defended tabletop escarpment and well-watered borders, held on into the tenth century, well after many of her sister cities had long perished.

Could endemic warfare really have done this? It's possible. One need think only of the great wars known to Europe's own bloody history. The Peloponnesian War, the Thirty Years' War, and the Hundred Years' War all depopulated huge swaths of the contested lands. The Classic Maya wars, stop-and-start though they were, lasted from 560 to 800, two and half centuries of steadily escalating military violence. In addition, these conflicts took place amongst the delicate ecology of a tropical rainforest. We like to think of the Classic Maya of the Petén fighting brutal wars with stone tools in a house made of glass.

Certainly, this is a possibility. We have yet to demonstrate such a theory conclusively to ourselves, much less to our rightfully skeptical colleagues. Still, studying the ancient past from El Perú-*Waka'* does suggest a strange inversion. If this theory is correct, the old city died because the surrounding forests were cut down, yet today the ruined city serves to *protect* the surrounding forests. Deforestation encroaches at the far-flung edges of the old city, held off by the scholars, scientists, environmentalists, and locals based within the urban ruin. In the next few years, El Perú-*Waka'* becomes a candidate for listing as a UNESCO World Heritage Site, a United Nations certification that the area both requires and deserves protection by the world community. Such recognition would go far in opening up funds for protection and research within the Laguna del Tigre National Park. If the forest can be saved, the big cats, the macaws, and even crocodiles can be saved as well. We can save this one forest. In such a way, the ruined city below will protect the rainforest above.

We hope it will. At the end of our all-too-short field seasons, we pack and leave the city. Our trucks, laden with dirty gear and the artifacts recovered from our excavations, tilt and wobble as they grind down the jungle path. The scattered ruins of El Perú-*Waka'* fall away, bit by bit. The piles of grass-covered debris and buried houses become less common as we make our way to the edge of the park. The shriek of the macaws lessens with distance. Maybe, from some heavy shadow, a big cat watches us go with lazy, disinterested eyes.

Digging Deep: A Hauntology of Cape Town

NICK SHEPHERD

Slave memory and branded coffee at the Truth Café. (Photo by Christian Ernsten.)

Earlier this year *The New York Times* named Cape Town as number one of "52 Places To Go in 2014". A short entry, placed below a dazzling photograph of Table Mountain, spoke to the reinvention of the city after apartheid. Readers were invited to: "Witness a city in transformation, glimpse exotic animals, explore the past and enjoy that beach before the crowds". As a long-time Capetonian I was proud to see my adoptive city featured in this way. At the same time, I realized that there was a lot that *The New York Times* was leaving out. By many accounts, Cape Town remains the most racially segregated city in South Africa. Perhaps more than any other South African city it presents scenes of stark contrast between great wealth and absolute poverty. The palatial homes of the Atlantic seaboard coexist with tin shacks lacking running water and basic sanitation. The blink of an eye takes you from one to the other. Every winter Cape Town's vast shacklands are flooded by the relentless rain and the rising water table. That such scenes of human misery should be set in a landscape of often awesome natural beauty only sharpens the contradiction.

My own relationship with the city remains ambivalent after thirty years. I find it a beautiful, frustrating, scary, inspiring, liberating place to live. When I am away I miss it. I never return without a sinking feeling in my stomach. "Back into the pressure cooker" I say to myself, as the plane lines up for its final approach. I came to Cape Town as a seventeen year-old to study archaeology at the University of Cape Town. Aside from short periods living in Europe and the United States it has been my home ever since. My memories of those early years are bound up with images of intense political activism in the dying days of apartheid. Paradoxically it was a time of great hope. We were young and we were remaking the world. Since then I have had to modify my dreams and expectations. It turns out that history does not turn a corner just because we want it to, that social and political processes are more complex than we had imagined, and that the past is both more vulnerable and more tenacious than we had credited.

In my recent work, I have tried to use archaeology – the discipline of which I am a part – to understand better the city in which I live. One of the compelling images that archaeology gives us is the image of the city as palimpsest; that is, as a layering of memory, experience and materiality. Often this exists as a literal layering of remains in the ground. Dig in any part of the historical city and you are likely to encounter the remains of other times, other versions of the city. In place of a surface reading of it we are encouraged to encounter the city differently, through the lens of accumulated experience and its material effects in the present. What follows is an attempt to do just that, via the story of the contested exhumation of an early colonial ground in a part of Cape Town called Green Point between

2003–4, and the events that followed. At one level, it is a story about Cape Town and its contemporary status and meaning. More deeply, it is a story about the discipline of archaeology, and about the kinds of choices that we are presented with as archaeologists. Deeper still, it is a story of self-discovery, as part of the ongoing conversation that I have with the place in which I live, and the discipline of which I am a part. In one important aspect *The New York Times* story was correct: Cape Town is a city busy reinventing itself, although this is not always in the direction that one might imagine.

Our story begins in the 1700s, during the period of Dutch occupation, when the area to the north and west of the growing town was the site of a number of formal and informal burial grounds, including the notorious "White Sands". Those interred in the informal burial grounds included a cross-section of the underclass of colonial Cape Town: slaves, free-blacks, artisans, fishermen, sailors, maids, washerwomen and their children, as well as executed criminals, suicides, paupers, and the unidentified victims of shipwrecks. In the 1820s this area – District One – was divided up for real estate and re-named Green Point. Later still, light industry moved into the area, and it fell into disrepair. In the late 1960s and early 1970s, black and Coloured residents of the inner city, working-class neighbourhood of Green Point were forcibly removed under the terms of the infamous Group Areas Act, a form of ethnic cleansing carried out by the apartheid state. In the property boom of 2000–2008 Green Point was reborn as "De Waterkant", part of the city's glitzy international zone and a centre of "pink Cape Town".

In May 2003, in the course of construction activities at a city block in Prestwich Street, Green Point, human remains were uncovered. The developer notified the South African Heritage Resources Agency (SAHRA) in accordance with the newly passed National Heritage Resources Act, and construction was halted. An archaeological contractor was appointed to handle the management of the site, and to run a public consultation process. At the same time, exhumation of the site was begun and the first bodies were removed. Three public meetings were held, in which it became apparent that there was considerable opposition to the exhumations. People questioned who would benefit from them, and why archaeological protocols were given precedence in the management of the site. Mavis Smallberg, a staff member from the Robben Island Museum, said:

my strong suggestion is to cover up the graves... Apart [from] the recently renamed Slave Lodge, there is no other public space that respectfully marks or memorializes the presence of slaves and the poor in Cape Town society... Only scientists are going to benefit from picking over these bones. Of what purpose and use is it to the various communities to which the dead belong to know what they ate 150 years ago or where they came from?

On 9 August the synod of the Cape Town diocese of the Anglican Church, under the leadership of Archbishop Njongonkulu Ndungane, the successor to Desmond Tutu, unanimously passed a resolution condemning the exhumations and calling for "[our] government, through its heritage agency... to maintain the integrity of the site as that of a cemetery".

One of the hallmarks of the public process around Prestwich Street was the passionate testimony given from the floor. At the second public meeting an unnamed respondent said:

there are multiple implications for this burial ground and its naked openness in the centre of the city... in this city there's never been a willingness to take up the issue of genocide and the destruction of human communities that were brought from across the globe... This is an opportunity to get to the bottom of that and time means different things to different people, institutions, stakeholders. Time for the dead: we need to consider what that means.

The Anglican minster, Michael Wheeder, who was later to play a central role in the organized opposition to the exhumations said:

Many of us of slave descent cannot say "here's my birth certificate". We are part of the great unwashed of Cape Town... The black people, we rush into town on the taxis and we need to rush out of town. At a time many decades ago we lived and loved and labored here. Nothing [reminds us of that history]... and so leave [the site] as a memorial to Mr. Gonzalez that lived there, Mrs. de Smidt that lived there. The poor of the area: the fishermen, the domestic workers, the people that swept the streets here. Memorialize that. Leave the bones there... That is a site they have owned for the first time in their lives *het hulle stukkie grond* [they have a little piece of ground]. Leave them in that ground. Why find now in the gentility of this new dispensation a place with which they have no connection?

On September 1st 2003, despite a clear weight of public opinion opposed to the exhumations, Pumla Madiba, the CEO of SAHRA, announced that archaeological work at the site would continue. She is reported as saying: "Many of the people who objected were highly emotional and did not give real reasons why the skeletons should not be relocated [*sic*]". On September 4th, the Hands Off Prestwich Street Committee was launched. At this point opposition to the exhumations shifted outside the officially mandated process of public consultation, to civil society and the politics of mass action. On September 12th the Hands Off Committee lodged an appeal with SAHRA calling for a halt to the exhumations and "a full and extended process of community consultation". The appeal document argues that "[exhumation] makes impossible a whole range of people's identifications with that specific physical space in the city. Such a removal echoes, albeit unintentionally, the apartheid regime's forced removals from the same area". The Hands Off Committee drew on anti-apartheid "struggle" tactics to draw attention to their cause. They organized regular candle-lit vigils at the Prestwich Street site on Sunday evenings. A billboard was erected outside St George's Cathedral in central Cape Town, a symbolic site of anti-apartheid protest, with the slogan: "Stop the exhumations! Stop the desecration!" Lunchtime pickets were held in the city centre. The appeal to SAHRA was turned down, as was a subsequent appeal to the Minister of Arts and Culture. Terry Lester of the Hands Off Committee is reported as saying: "We're acting the whore in this instance, bowing down to the god of development and selling a segment of our history".

Over two thousand bodies were exhumed from the Prestwich Street site. These were stored in a warehouse adjacent to the site. On 21 April 2004 – Freedom Day in South Africa – the remains were ceremonially transferred from the Prestwich Street site to the mortuary of Woodstock Day Hospital, on the other side of the city. Some of the remains were carried in procession through the city centre in eleven flag-draped boxes, one for each of the official language groups in the country. Later still, they were transferred to a purpose-built "ossuary" on the edge of Green Point, named the New Prestwich Memorial Building. With the construction of the Cape Town Stadium in Green Point as part of the preparations for the 2010 FIFA World Cup, this unpromising site was reconfigured through it adjacency to a "fan walk", laid out from the centre of the city to the new stadium. The dead of Prestwich Street, in their restless transit of the postapartheid city, were brought into a new set of relationships: this time with the tens of thousands of football fans who walked in mass procession to watch the big games.

Prestwich Street has been the most contested instance of archaeological work in South Africa in the period since the elections of 1994. In thinking through the events around Prestwich Street, I have been interested in three things. The first is what they can tell us about Cape Town and South Africa, two decades after the official end of apartheid. The second is what they can tell us about the state of archaeology. The third is what they can tell us about questions of history and representation in the wake of what political philosopher Anthony Bogues has called "historical catastrophe". Regarding the first: clearly much more was at stake at Prestwich Street than the final disposition of the dead, important as such an issue might be. Opposition to the exhumations came from a number of quarters: slave-descended Capetonians, Khoisan First Nations activists, Christian and Muslim faith leaders, community activists, and left-leaning scholars. Centrally at play were issues of rights, resources, representation and restitution after apartheid. Following the visual historian Elizabeth Edwards, I have been drawn to regard Prestwich as a "point of fracture"; that is, a set of events through which we might glimpse the working out of a range of forces and interests in post-apartheid society. These forces and interests have to do with questions of history and memory, but they also have to do with issues of citizenship, the possibilities and limitations of participatory politics, and the emergent shape and nature of a post-apartheid public sphere. In a dramatically metaphorical, but also in an entirely literal fashion, the eruption of the Prestwich Street dead into the fabric of post-apartheid society set off a chain of events that confront us with the unfinished business of the past, and are as revealing as they are discomforting.

Neither was Prestwich Street alone in this regard. In October 2003, just as archaeological work was resuming on the Prestwich Street site in the wake of the third public meeting, the remains of over 400 Africans were being reinterred on the site of the African Burial Ground in Lower Manhattan, New York City. This followed a long and passionately fought campaign on the part of an African-American descendent community, around control of the research process, forms of memorialization, and the final disposition of the dead. The story of the African Burial Ground is deservedly well known in archaeological circles, less so the story of Prestwich Street, yet the parallels between the two sites are striking. It is significant that in both cases the re-emergence of the ancestral dead became an opportunity whereby socially marginalized groups were able to stake a claim and make their voices heard. I have argued that this constitutes an important idiom for a politics "from below", which directly implicates archaeology and archaeologists. The very materiality of archaeological sites and remains makes them powerful points of mobilization, organization and identification, particularly when refracted through ties of culture, identity and descent. In a media-saturated era of what cultural theorist Stuart Hall has called the "global postmodern", characterized by disembodied experience and deterritorialization, archaeological sites and remains provide powerful points of counter identification. It is characteristic both of this era and of the state of the discipline that some of the most politically contested contexts of contemporary archaeological practice are concerned with the repatriation and restitution of human remains.

At both Prestwich Street and the African Burial Ground a subaltern politics emerged, as it were, "at the sharp edge of the trowel". In both cases, archaeologists close to the events were deeply divided in their responses. I was among a small number of archaeologists and historians in South Africa who were opposed to the exhumations and broadly supportive of the aims of the Hands Off Committee. Most archaeologists were supportive of the actions of SAHRA and the archaeological contractors working the site, and took speedy, total exhumation as a given. They argued in terms of the value of the site as a research opportunity and a source of "hidden histories". Archaeologist Belinda Mutti argued in favor of exhumation "to give history back to the people". Liesbet Schiettecatte argued that "[leaving] bones leaves information unknown. Studying them brings them back to life…" Such arguments reference the South African historical archaeology of the 1980s, and are both persuasive and sincere in their intention. However, they need to be set aside when the very "people" to whom one is proposing "to give history back" are opposed to archaeological intervention. For many of the anti-exhumation protesters, such statements unconsciously echoed colonial science, with its assumptions around rights of access and ownership.

Of more interest to me was the manner in which the activists of the Hands Off Committee articulated and mobilized a counter discourse, both as a way of conceptualizing their own relationship to the remains, and as a way of mounting a public and legal challenge to the exhumations. In public statements, submissions, and appeals they emphasized the language of memory, experience, and empathetic identification. They sought to articulate an alternative set of values, and alternative notions of space and time. This included notions of the site as a site of memory and conscience rather than an archaeological site, and in one memorable intervention, the notion of "time for the dead". Most of all, they contested the notion of a distanced and objectified past, whose relationship with the present is mediated by expert knowledge. In their own more complexly imagined version of this relationship, the re-emergence of the Prestwich Street dead in the world of the living is not described through the trope of discovery and revelation, but rather as a "learning moment".

As part of a counter discourse around Prestwich Street, I saw some powerful proposals around forms of memorialization. Hannah Mintz, a student in Brown University's Public Humanities program proposed leaving the site of interment with its remains in the ground as an open, green space in an increasingly densely constructed urban environment: a place to hang out, eat lunch, bring the kids or snooze in the sun. In my own work I wrote in favor of the notion of an "archaeology of silence". This is premised on the idea that our generation – the first generation after apartheid – stands to learn more by leaving the remains in the ground and starting a conversation around the implications of their "naked openness in the city", than by exhuming them and subjecting them to disciplinary procedures. For us, the "learning moment" is not about imagined pasts sequestered in deep time, but about the far more urgent and difficult matter of how it is that we meet one another as South Africans who stand on opposite sides of a divided history.

This brings us to questions of history and representation. I have in front of me a glossy brochure for "The Rockwell: luxury De Waterkant living". The Rockwell, which was constructed on the Prestwich Street site, consists of 103 "New York-style" apartments, plus parking bays, a private gym, a restaurant, a deli, and a swimming pool. The historical point of reference for the development is the Harlem Renaissance, or as the brochure has it, New York's "Jazz Age". According to the brochure: "Inspired by the early 1900 buildings of downtown Manhattan, The Rockwell displays an inherent richness and warmth". This is because "At the turn of the previous century, they did design right. Not only because it was classical in form and function… But because they did it with soul". Doing it "with soul" becomes a refrain, and the rest of the brochure makes reference to "Rock and Soul", "Pure Soul", "Rich Soul", "Style and Soul", and "Rhythm and Soul". The accompanying images show clean, depopulated interiors dusted free of history, unwelcome associations, and the stain of the earth below. I admit to a certain bewilderment. How do we interpret this, other than as the annihilation of history and local memory? Is The Rockwell a nod in the direction of the African Burial Ground? Or is the Harlem Renaissance invoked merely for its associations with cool in an otherwise uncool environment? The full weight of the phrase "forced removals" strikes home. I think: the Hands Off Committee were correct to see the connection between historical slavery at the Cape and the living memory of forced removals. I think: at Prestwich Street we see the instantiation of a new kind of post-apartheid historical imaginary, in which history is imagined by the victors and beneficiaries, and in which victims have no place.

If The Rockwell suggests a loosening of the forms of historical representation and the bonds of obligation that bind the present and the past, then subsequent events confirm this. Faced with the challenge of making the

New Prestwich Memorial Building economically sustainable, the Cape Town City Council turned over most of the public space of the memorial for the establishment of a coffee shop. The website *bizcommunity.com* reports: "Charismatic leader and coffee evangelist David Donde launched his new coffee brand and café, Truth Coffeecult, on Wednesday 24th March 2010, at the Prestwich Memorial". Truth Coffeecult's own website invites you "to experience the simple elegance of micro-lots of artisanal roasted relationship coffees prepared by geek baristas". It continues: "Not all coffees are created equal. At Truth, the bitter horror of the over-roasted bean is avoided… Experience Truth. Coffee as religion". The Truth Café references South Africa's Truth and Reconciliation Commission of the late-1990s, presided over by Archbishop Desmond Tutu. Those somber and significant events are reprised as a hymn in praise of coffee. Baristas at the Truth Café wear T-shirts with the legend "Truth". At the cash register one is invited to give "Tips for Truth". A recent promotion invites you to: "Get a free cup of Truth". In a more direct set of references, coffee grinders at the Truth Café bear the image of a human skull crossed by the letter "T", and stacked cardboard boxes of coffee beans reference the stacked boxes of human remains in the vault next door. Visit the Truth Café on an average day and you will find city-centre hipsters, tourists, and members of Green Point's boho elite sipping coffee, taking advantage of the free wifi, and enjoying Cape Town's fickle weather.

In his major work of the mid-1990s, the French poststructuralist theorist Jacques Derrida introduces the notion of the "specter", which he describes as that which history has repressed (*Specters of Marx: The State of the Debt, the Work of Mourning, and the New International*, 1994). He develops this idea via the notion of a "hauntology" (a near-homophone to "ontology" in French), which might be loosely translated as an account of disavowed terms, absent presences, and spectral remains. For Derrida, hauntology resonates with the notion of "revenants", the act of return, and the kind of disjunctive temporalities that are captured in the phrase "the time is out of joint". I have come to understand Cape Town as a city haunted by the legacies of the past, and the specters of unfinished business. More than that, I have come to understand Cape Town as a city characterized by strangely disjunctive temporalities, poised between catastrophic pasts and glibly imagined futures.

Over the past two decades, Cape Town has acquired much of the paraphernalia of a world city of a certain kind: a waterfront, a convention centre, a world heritage site, a natural wonder of the world, themed shopping malls, blue-flag beaches, backpacker precincts, gated communities, safari outfits, overland adventures, poverty tourism, and a rapidly expanding study-abroad infrastructure that interfaces with colleges in the United States. In many cases, these developments are scaffolded on the blueprint of the apartheid city, so that the old and the new exist alongside, sometimes on top of, one another. This temporal disjuncture is expressed spatially, so that a short journey will take you from an unreconstructed apartheid township to the perfumed galleries of the Constantia Mall, or the "Victoria and Albert Waterfront", themed to evoke the world of Queen Victoria and her consort. In these charmed spaces one encounters the past as nostalgia, and the specters are banished for as long as it takes to swipe a charge card or order a second cup of coffee ("Make mine a Truth"). We might develop this thought by saying that in the contested public sphere of the postcolony there is a certain kind of pleasure that is premised on institutionalized forgetting. Or we might put this differently, by saying that for those who can afford it the ultimate holiday lies in taking a holiday from history.

What Prestwich Street reminds us is that the past is not so easily put behind us, that specters are not so summarily laid to rest, and that the dead are not so conveniently forgotten. The sudden return of the revenant, the eruption of the ancestral dead into the space of the postcolony, breaks the spell of forgetfulness. It reminds us of what the poor and disenfranchised have always known, that for most people there are no holidays from history. Anthony Bogues's notion of historical catastrophe is premised on the idea not of the singular traumatic event in the past that we relate to through an act of memory, but rather on the idea that catastrophic events recapitulate through time, that their effects are borne on the bodies of their subjects, that the real trauma is that they condition our present and not just our past. For Cape Town's victims of forced removal, the catastrophe lies not only in the original act of removal from city centre to outlying township, but in the fact that for every day that follows they must recapitulate this removal in their journey to and from work. For Michael Wheeder of the Hands Off Committee, this is what was at stake in asserting a claim to a little piece of ground in the city centre.

If the notion of historical catastrophe suggests a certain kind of entrapment of the poor, and if my notion of "holidays from history" suggests a way in which forgetfulness becomes a commodity, available to those who can afford it, then the idea that I have been working towards is that Cape Town as a city is designed to ease us into this kind of differentiated urban experience. This may be its true nature as a "world" city and the sense in which it speaks to global trends, or even has a kind of predictive capacity, for while it is surely not alone in this regard, in Cape Town we see the apotheosis of a certain kind of easeful living, carried out in the midst of misery. The gated communities, the beaches, the malls: it may not be enough to say "I live in Cape Town", but rather "In which Cape Town do I live?" Prestwich Street holds up a mirror to our sense of ourselves and our sense of the city. It also holds up a mirror to the discipline of archaeology. I have one final line of enquiry, but for that I need to climb a mountain.

It's Sunday morning, a lovely, clear day. I decide to walk to Peers Cave. I call the kids and load up the car. As an afterthought, I call the dog ("Angel", a sweet natured family pet). A short drive takes us to the base of the hill on which Peers Cave is situated, in the Fish Hoek valley, about half an hour due south of the city. Peers Cave is a large and impressive rock shelter that at one time contained a substantial archaeological deposit. The walk to Peers Cave takes you over some sand dunes and up a steep, sandy slope. My eldest, Rosa, leads the way. Felix, aged six, scrambles to catch up. My middle child, Giles, walks beside me, chatting about what he sees. Angel lags.

Peers Cave was excavated in the 1920s by a father-and-son team from Fish Hoek called Victor and Bertie Peers. Their excavation methods were crude. They used dynamite to shift the larger boulders. In the language of the day they were described as "enthusiasts". Victor and Bertie Peers exhumed a large number of human remains from the cave, including a number of infant burials. One adult skeleton achieved renown as the so-called "Fish Hoek Man". When members of the British Association for the Advancement of Science arrived in Cape Town in 1929 for a convention, they climbed the hill to Peers Cave, a pilgrimage to the home of Fish Hoek Man. I am thinking about writing a book about Peers Cave. The Peers father and son ransacked the site, but this may be too obvious a way in. What I am really interested in is the relationship between the cave on the hill and the settlement in the valley. Fish Hoek was laid out as a suburb in 1918. With its radial street plan, its proximity to the ocean, and its rail link to the city centre, it promoted itself to a growing white middle class as a model town on the urban periphery. Until at least the 1970s, Peers Cave and the Fish Hoek Man formed a strong part of the mythology of Fish Hoek. My imagination tracks between the dead hunter-gatherers, the dynamite, and the model apartheid citizens in their settlement in the valley.

At last we're there. The view from the top is spectacular. The kids fan out. The dog finds a patch of shade. I sit on a rock: I need to think. In the late-1990s and early-2000s – before the events around Prestwich Street – I wrote a series of papers in which I argued for the notion of a postcolonial archaeology, which I envisaged would be an archaeology for the people. The effect of colonialism and apartheid had been to divorce archaeology from popular aspirations and concerns. Many South African archaeologists had taken refuge in the scientism and empiricism of the New Archaeology, and had argued that the social contexts of archaeological practice were none of their concern. I argued that we now had the opportunity to address this state of affairs. However, at the time that I was writing the seeds of a different kind of future were already taking root. Around this time two sets of forces were transforming worlds of practice in archaeology, not just in South Africa but globally, and both were present at Prestwich Street. The first was the global rise and ascendency of contract archaeology and a discourse on cultural resource management. The second was the growth of the Indigenous Movement, and of a politics of identity articulated around archaeological sites and remains.

In many contexts, the effects of the rise of contract archaeology have been nothing short of profound. Archaeologists of my generation have seen the discipline transformed, literally before our eyes. In South Africa, as in many other countries, the vast majority of archaeological work is now carried out under the aegis of contract archaeology. There has been a significant reduction both in the total number of research-led archaeological projects, and in the proportion of research-led archaeology versus contract archaeology. More pointedly for the discipline, there has also been a reorientation of accountabilities and lines of reporting. Rather than the forms of popular accountability that some of us were arguing for, this has been in the direction of corporate accountability and the bureaucratization of heritage management processes. Ironically, contract archaeology made its appearance in South Africa in the very period of political transition, when many people were sensing a new openness in public life.

If the rise of contract archaeology implies the truncation of a certain kind of potential, then the second set of developments have been more engaging and more positive (or so I would argue). The growth of the Indigenous Movement and of a self-conscious politics of memory and identity articulated around archaeological sites and remains has framed a challenge to traditional notions of expertise and authority, and to established expectations around access and ownership in archaeology. For many of us it has constituted what the Hands Off Committee described as a "learning moment". The result has been an important set of debates that have introduced a new reflexivity and thoughtfulness into archaeological practice in many contexts. Many of us now understand archaeology to be a form of disciplinary practice that is negotiated at the intersection of multiple interests. Sub-fields like Public Archaeology and Indigenous Archaeology give expression to this understanding that many of the old taken-for-granteds no longer apply.

Prestwich Street was remarkable in that, as well as a politics-from-below, it presented what might be described as an "epistemology-from-below". The core challenge of the Hands Off Committee was not only around questions of access and ownership, but also around questions of knowledge and the terms of engagement. In framing alternative notions of time, place and personhood they were questioning the nature of disciplinary knowledge, and the terms of the relationship between the past and the present (or the living and the dead). I have argued that such epistemologies-from-below offer a tremendous opportunity for the renewal of archaeology. It is by attending to – by really attending to – these articulated knowledge worlds that we begin to decolonize disciplinary epistemologies. It is fitting and appropriate that in many instances, the site of the production of theory in archaeology has shifted outside of the academy and into the life-worlds of descendent and affected communities. I would understand that theory in archaeology now takes place as a conversation between the academy and such life-worlds.

I would never claim to speak for the dead of Prestwich Street, nor do I any longer believe that I am in the business of "giving history back to the people", as I might have done as a younger man. My sense of myself, and of my place in the city and in the discipline is conditioned by an altogether more humble realization: it is the question of what it means to dwell in this place together with the dead of Prestwich Street. Their presence and being conditions my own being in the city. I want to think about what this awareness of time and materiality means for my own practice as an archaeologist. I want to think about how archaeology opens out to a new awareness of time and materiality. In my future practice I will continue to work with social movements. I also want to broaden my disciplinary collaborations, to work with video and performance artists, photographers, curators. I want to experiment with writing fiction. I pluck some words out of the air: performance, embodiment, materiality, co-presence. What an exciting time to be an archaeologist!

Time to walk back down the hill. I call the kids. The dog has run off somewhere. Together we shout: "Angel! Angel…"

— 9 —

Eating in Uronarti

Laurel Bestock

The site of Uronarti, looking south.
(Kite aerial photograph by L. Bestock and C. Knoblauch.)

Uronarti, which means "island of the king" in Nubian, is the site of an Egyptian fortress in the northern part of northern Sudan. This stretch of the Nile was conquered by the Egyptians nearly 4000 years ago, and they built monumental fortresses of sun-dried brick that dominated the landscape, the gold-bearing deserts, the trade corridor that was the river, the people who lived here.

In the 1960s the waters of the Nile rose to form the world's largest man-made lake behind the Aswan High Dam. Egyptian prerogatives imposed themselves on this landscape again, local populations were moved, north and south. The past of this borderland was erased by the lake, which covered countless archaeological sites. Only very recently was it realized that two of the Egyptian fortresses were above the waterline – places to which one could return to ask new questions about old colonial interactions.

Working at Uronarti is a challenge, because it is remote. The nearest real town, Wadi Halfa, is 50 km and several hours away. The population of Uronarti itself consists of Zakaria, who built a hut on the southernmost promontory and who fishes year-round, and an extended family that lives elsewhere but whose men come to farm on weekends, sometimes for longer. Lutfi and Saif, members of this family, were born on Uronarti before the lake rose, and now teach school in Wadi Halfa. Yasser and Ali, from farther away, stay weeks or months at a time. Goat herders sometimes drive their flocks through, but do not stay.

It is only the lake that has made fishing, farming, and grazing possible. Before the dam this stretch of river was inhospitable, characterized by rapids tumbling through granite narrows, with almost no floodplain, almost nothing green. The last decade has seen a drop of several meters in the level of the lake, and the rich silt that settled from the now placid waters – the same silt that was the engine of ancient Egyptian agriculture – allows plants to grow. The island is only an island at high water, now, and at most times of year one can walk to the west bank.

Food is a constant ordering principal of our lives in Uronarti, and that we must spend so much time planning it, procuring it, preparing it, has opened us to thoughts about how people ate here in the past. Documenting food and the human relationships around it has become an important part of the archaeological project for me.

Produce seller in the Wadi Halfa souk.

Boy washing vegetables to sell in Wadi Halfa.

Shadia, our inspector, buying lentils, rice, and pasta in Wadi Halfa. All our dry goods, our bread, our oil, and our cooking gas canisters, come from Halfa.

The northern section of the fortress. The square rooms are granaries. The grain for the garrison was shipped from Egypt. Grain was also currency, and the storage capacity of these granaries is much greater than we think was needed to support the population living here. (Kite aerial photograph by L. Bestock and K. Howley.)

Ian making morning tea over a fire, when our gas had run out. The fortress is in the background, on the hill behind Ian.

Zakaria in his fishing boat.

Eggplant growing near site.

Zakaria's hut, built partly of fishing nets, on the southern part of the island. Fish strung to dry can be seen just behind the hut on the left.

Lutfi and Saif irrigating the *fuul* (fava beans) on the weekend.

Shadia cuts a watermelon brought by Yasser.

Ali makes *gurassa*, somewhere between a pancake and a bread, while giving us a lesson in Nubian.

Fuul, salad, and stale bread.

Goat herders watch to make sure their flock does not eat the *fuul.*

Christian and Ian prepare dinner by headlamp.

A goat leg suspended from Yasser's *khema*. The rest of the goat was cooked for us as a celebratory meal.

Shadia and Christian drawing cooking pots. Most ancient ceramics on Uronarti are Egyptian, but the presence of Nubian cooking pots indicates that this was a place of cultural interaction.

Roadside food vendors on the trip to Khartoum at the end of the season.

Who Are the People?

Susan E. Alcock, J. Andrew Dufton,
and Müge Durusu-Tanriöver

Word cloud showing frequency (represented by size) of terms mentioned in response to the survey question "Why should anyone care about archaeology?"

In 2013 and 2014, Brown University presented two iterations of *Archaeology's Dirty Little Secrets* (or ADLS), one of its three pilot MOOCs (Massive Open Online Courses) offered on the Coursera platform. The class was designed by the three authors of this chapter, with Alcock as the lead instructor, and Dufton and Durusu-Tanrıöver as Teaching Assistants. Taken together, the two classes had an initial enrolment of over 63,000 people; over 30,000 people actively engaged with course materials in more than 150 countries (see figures on pp. 132–133). ADLS was the first, and still one of the very few, MOOCs to focus on the discipline of archaeology. Its favorable and grateful reception, we argue, reinforces this volume's arguments: first, that archaeology possesses enormous popular appeal, and second, that archaeologists too often fail to communicate effectively with their broadest potential audience.

The initial announcement of the *Archaeology for the People* competition, which happened shortly after the launch of ADLS, led us to return to these people who had found archaeology sufficiently appealing – or compelling – to pursue the class. Through the use of an online anonymous and completely voluntary questionnaire, to be discussed further below, we asked a variety of questions exploring their curiosity about, and attitudes toward, the field. Far from being a mere exercise in exploring our "fan base," our ambition was to identify the modes, times, and places in which people seem best to discover and follow archaeology, and to envision ways to help them do so more effectively, more ethically, and more enjoyably.

We are the first to admit that our results rest on a biased and partial sample, in some ways preaching to an already converted choir. But if this volume seeks to articulate a better Archaeology for the People, we argue these are – in the first instance – the interested and motivated people to bear in mind. In other words, flawed though the sample is, it offers one bottom-up, grassroots view of what people make of archaeology, and of how they want to learn more.

Archaeology's Dirty Little Secrets: An Overview

Coursera's format has certain established sections for each course home-page: a short "blurb," a list of prerequisites and resources needed, and an answer to the question, "What is the coolest thing I'll learn if I take this class?" Our blurb for ADLS summed up our ambitions:

> Admit it – you wanted to be an archaeologist when you grew up... This course builds on that enthusiasm, while radically expanding your notions about just what archaeology is and just what archaeologists do.

Our only prerequisite was "Just be curious"; the only resources needed "Computer, internet connection, and a willingness to do some odd things"; our answer to the "coolest thing" query was "You will never look at the ground in the same way again." The dirty little secrets in question ranged from the latent biases (gold, digging, mummies, Indiana Jones) that run rampant in the popular imagination, to more profound issues, such as presentation of the past in museum settings, or the worldwide and accelerating destruction of cultural heritage. Time was spent on what takes place "out" of the field as well as in it, and on conveying the sheer breadth of people and institutions involved in archaeological practice.

The class lasted for eight weeks (or "units"), unveiling on a weekly basis new content filmed in various locations across the Brown University campus. Over the course of these eight units, we introduced people to the various stages of archaeological projects, as well as to the spectrum of skills and activities involved in the discipline. Weekly segments included "Office Hours" in which Alcock introduced key themes in her extremely messy, but pedagogically useful, office; more standard lectures; conversations with Brown faculty about ongoing fieldwork as it pertained to the unit theme; hands-on demonstrations of working with various object and material types; and short screen-casts exploring archaeological People, Places and Things from across the globe. Assignments included both automated unit quizzes checking for basic understanding of weekly content, and archaeological exercises, peer-graded by other students taking the class, ranging from creating three-dimensional models of artifacts with a cell phone to the composition of archaeological "Bucket Lists". Our aim with ADLS, from the beginning, was to be inclusive – no prior knowledge was expected and all course materials were freely available online– and to communicate the collaborative excitement and teamwork orientation of archaeology to as broad and varied an audience as possible.

We have discussed elsewhere in detail the structure of this course, its successes and challenges (Alcock et al. forthcoming). With completion rates higher than normal for MOOCs and with an enthusiastic community whose online discussions proved nearly as productive and interactive as brick-and-mortar classrooms, ADLS to a great extent accomplished what it set out to do: to get people energized about archaeology by building on their own interests and, in some cases, misconceptions, and to show them avenues for further engagement with the discipline (Table 1).

As already noted at the start of this chapter, ADLS reached tens of thousands of people. The only characteristics shared across this entire group were, by definition, that these were individuals who could understand English fairly well, and who had internet access. Otherwise, the class proved to be a crazy quilt. Class members, of which there were more women than men,

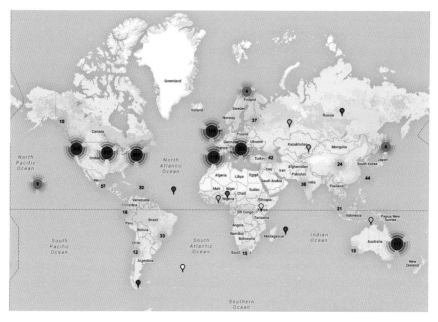

Voluntary, participant-generated map showing the international distribution of ADLS course participants in 2013. (In areas with a dense concentration of respondents, total numbers of students are represented in the center of each cluster.)

	2013	2014
Enrolled students	40728	22727
Active students	18291	12370

			Activity as % of active students	
			2013	2014
Watched a video	17276	10951	94.45%	88.53%
Completed an assessment (quiz or written)	9747	4836	53.29%	39.09%
Browsed discussion forums	9866	6442	53.94%	52.08%
Received completion certificate	3026	1267	16.54%	10.24%

Table 1. Breakdown of student enrolment, activity, and completion for 2013 and 2014 offerings of *Archaeology's Dirty Little Secrets*.

ranged in age from younger than 10 to over 80. The majority had at least some college experience. Some worked full-time; some were retired; some unemployed. Some were expatriates; some were house-bound through illness or family obligations; some were home-schooled. Some were archaeologists

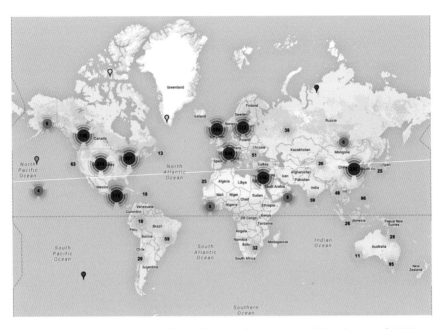

Voluntary, participant-generated map showing the international distribution of ADLS course participants in 2014. (In areas with a dense concentration of respondents, total numbers of students are represented in the center of each cluster.)

themselves; some had archaeologists in the family; some had wanted to be archaeologists; some want to be archaeologists. Some completed the course (entailing several hours of work each week); some watched what they could when they could and left it at that.

We know these demographics and details because over 13,000 people were willing either to fill out Coursera's voluntary anonymous course surveys or to speak openly about their experiences in the busy ADLS discussion forums. Postings also continue to the *Archaeology's Dirty Little Secrets* Facebook page with, at present, over 7,000 "likes." Even if these exchanges of information inevitably leave many of the people who followed the class invisible to us, we have – at least impressionistically – a sense of who some of them are.

We invited this group – all active participants of ADLS 2013 and 2014 and our Facebook followers – to fill out an informal and anonymous questionnaire (Table 2). To our profound gratitude, 2,675 individuals responded. This was never intended to be a sophisticated survey instrument that would quantitatively break down particular answers by particular demographic category (country of residence, gender, age, level of education, etc.) What we can do is speak to the international demographics of those

	Question	Answer Options
1	Did you participate in Archaeology's Dirty Little Secrets (ADLS) Coursera course? (Select all that apply)	• Participated in 2013 • Participated in 2014 • I did not participate
2	If you participated in ADLS, have you followed up the course by learning about or doing more archaeology in any way? (Select one)	• Yes • No
3	How old were you when you became interested in archaeology? (Select one)	Select one: 0–9, 10–17, 18–25, 26–45, 46–65, 66–75, 76–85, 85+
4	How would you describe your engagement with archaeology? (Select all that apply)	• I am interested in archaeology, but have no formal training • I have taken archaeology courses at university • I have taken archaeology courses online • I am a member of a local archaeological society • I have volunteered on an archaeological project with a local museum • I am a professional archaeologist or curator • Other
5	How often do you read materials relating to archaeology? (Select one)	• Never • Less than once a month • Once a month • 2–3 times a month • Once a week • 2–3 times a week • Daily
6	What types of materials related to archaeology do you read? (Select all that apply)	• Print newspapers • Magazines • Popular publications • Academic publications • Archaeological/historical fiction • Online content (websites, blogs, etc.)
7	What is your favorite book or article about archaeology? Why?	(Open ended question)
8	Do you follow any archaeologists on social media? (Select one)	• Yes • No
9	If yes, who?	(Open ended question)
10	What social media platforms do you use to follow archaeologists or discover archaeological information? (Select all that apply)	• Facebook • Twitter • Google Plus • Instagram • Pinterest • Flickr • LinkedIn • Academia.edu • Other
11	How important and effective are media other than printed texts (videos, pictures, audio, etc.) in the dissemination of archaeological information? (Select one)	• Very important • Somewhat important • Neither important nor unimportant • Somewhat unimportant • Very unimportant

Table 2. A full list of survey questions and potential responses (continued p. 135).

12	How often do you visit archaeological sites or museums? (Select one)	• Never • Less than once a month • Once a month • 2–3 times a month • Once a week • 2–3 times a week • Daily
13	Have you ever volunteered or worked at an archaeological site or museum? (Select one)	• Yes • No
14	If yes, where?	(Open ended question)
15	If not, what things have stopped you from volunteering at an archaeological site or museum? (Select all that apply)	• Financial restrictions • Time restrictions • Family commitments • Not knowing about available opportunities • Other
16	Please rank these threats to archaeological heritage from most (1) to least (6) serious:	• Looting/vandalism • Armed conflict • Environmental damage • Development • Tourist traffic • Lack of funding for cultural heritage
17	Are you interested in archaeology to find out something about yourself and your past, or to learn about the past of somebody else?	(Open ended question)
18	Very briefly, why should anyone care about archaeology?	(Open ended question)
19	Do you have any other comments about ADLS, or the dissemination of archaeological information more generally?	(Open ended question)

Table 2, continued.

invited, and the country of residence of our respondents. The Anglophone communities of North America and the United Kingdom make up roughly half of our pool of questionnaire respondents. Cross-referencing these figures with the country of origin of the Internet Protocol (IP) addresses of those completing our survey shows the sample – perhaps expectedly for this kind of English-language questionnaire issued by an American university – skews toward American and Anglophone traditions (Table 3). Nonetheless, other nations, languages, and cultural traditions are also represented in 30% of our responses, or roughly 800 people. These contributions of non-American, non-Anglophone voices emerge in answers to specific survey questions. Although such a voluntary sampling method does not allow us to comment in more detail on the specific responses of a given gender, age, or other demographic group, intriguing patterns still emerge that bear consideration for thinking about the future of archaeological instruction and involvement.

Facebook		ADLS 2013		ADLS 2014		Survey respondents	
Country	% of users	Country	% of users	Country	% of users	Country	% of users
US	37	US	42	US	34	US	49.1
UK	7	UK	7	China	15	UK	9.7
India	4	India	5	UK	6	Canada	5.7
Canada	3	Canada	4	Canada	4	Australia	4.5
Spain	3	Brazil	3	India	3	Spain	3.7
Greece	3	Australia	3	Spain	3	Greece	2.2
Australia	3	Spain	3	Australia	3	Germany	1.6
Brazil	3	Greece	2	Russian Federation	2	Brazil	1.6
Egypt	2	Germany	2	Brazil	2	India	1.5
Mexico	2	China	2	Greece	2	France	1.4

Table 3. Comparison of top-ten countries of residence of ADLS Facebook "fans," ADLS 2013 and 2014 participants, and survey correspondents.

Patterns in the Population

First, and unsurprisingly, by far the vast majority of respondents had participated in ADLS, and some indeed followed the course twice. The questionnaire results, therefore, share the biases of the course population already described (more educated, more female, and more engaged) – observations that must be kept in mind for the discussion that follows. Very gratifying, if perhaps also not surprising, was the preponderance of people (some 73%) who, having taken the MOOC, said they had gone on to learn more, or even to do some archaeology.

Among professional archaeologists, it is something of a cliché to remark that many of us became addicted at a relatively early age (the senior author believes she was about six, Dufton eight, Durusu-Tanrıöver 13). To explore this, we asked how old people were when they became interested, breaking out the categories of choice to reflect widely shared – if by no means universal – educational stages. Here we followed the relatively standardized American framework which breaks approximately 12 years of study into two parts, ending at age 17–18 and followed either by college or early career stages. It is beyond our scope to explore the specifics of other countries and their variations on this general model, but we invite people to consider the results in light of other educational systems.

Support for the theory of archaeological "early adopters" is visible, with 23% reporting in Category 1 (ages 0–9), roughly the primary school years. Category 2 (ages 10–17), the middle and high school years, at 32% emerged as the most popular time to get hooked. It is frequently in the sixth grade (approximately age 11) that students in the United States are first formally exposed to study of the ancient world (Egypt, Mesopotamia, Greece, Rome), which often, if not always, introduces archaeology as a mode of exploration. Third most common, by a whisker, was Category 3 (ages 18–25) at 16%, representing the undergraduate college or early career years. Numbers tail off from there, though with heartening indications of lifelong learning and the development of new interests well past six score years and ten.

What implications can be drawn from this distribution? Most thought-provoking is the fact that over 50% of respondents were attracted to archaeology by the age of 18, a clarion signal that our field should target the young. Looking at the data more closely, early childhood emerged as a rich time for engagement, but given that (at least in the United States) those caught before the age of 10 are unlikely to have been exposed to the field in school, we must consider other vectors of transmission. Although one usual suspect is Indiana Jones, he is unlikely ever to have been the key to this particular demographic and – at least for today's young – his name-recognition is waning. It is more likely that children receive signals about the field from television or popular media more generally, suggesting that early impressions of archaeology are likely to revolve around the discipline's traditional stereotypes. The question thus becomes what could be done to capture that excitement and shape it more productively, especially as children move on in school.

The critical stage of years 10 to 17, in America the middle and high school years, must next be highlighted. At this point, we would hazard that a spike associated with the introductory teaching of ancient civilizations is far from accidental, which in turn raises serious concerns about the diminishing presence of history and social sciences for that age group, at least in the United States. At this age, it is also possible to convey more robust and responsible perceptions of archaeology, as well as using the field (with its intrinsic fascination already in place for many) as a platform for teaching a range of more general subjects and skills, not least in the STEM (Science, Technology, Engineering, and Mathematics) disciplines. This has been explored by a range of players – in the United States, for example, by the American Association for the Advancement of Science, and in the United Kingdom by MOLA (Museum of London Archaeology). It is clear, however, that there is enormous space for growth in addressing this crucial age group.

Others became switched on in the college years. In our personal experience, such students often report having had no opportunity to access the field earlier, owing to the nature of their school system or the priorities of their teachers. The bias thus introduced into just who gets to hear just what about archaeology is evident. College could be a prime time for exposure and, given the decline in the number of new adopters after the age of 25, archaeology would be wise to market itself aggressively on university campuses, and to find other forms of outreach beyond traditional educational structures. MOOCs are one way forward, we argue, but that yet begs the question of how we ensure that people are sufficiently intrigued to sign up if we miss these high-yield ages.

As for describing people's involvement with archaeology, by far the top choices were "I am interested in archaeology, but have no formal training" (68%) and "I have taken archaeology courses online" (49%) – again, a reflection of the sample's origin (note, people could indicate more than one option). Others had taken archaeology at university, were members of a local archaeological society, or had volunteered in some capacity. Individual comments threw up a remarkably varied landscape of specifics: writing about archaeology for an Argentinian magazine; being a member of a historical re-enactment society; doing tours such as Road Scholar; researching for a novel. Amusingly, one reported being the child of two archaeologists who strictly forbade her to study archaeology; less entertaining was the traveler who likes to buy real artifacts.

The prevailing trends among the free-form text answers here, however, force us to reconsider our own academic categories of "training", "research," and "engagement". Many respondents described their engagement as a matter of reading omnivorously and watching television: two answers we had failed even to offer as options for this specific question. It is clear that we are dealing with an audience demanding modes of engagement more varied and flexible than those we put forward (e.g., taking courses at university, belonging to an archaeological society). We must rethink both the nature and technologies of what constitutes archaeological outreach.

Patterns in Media Engagement

We explored this issue of engagement further, by asking how often people read in the area of archaeology (with less than once a month, once a month, and two to three times a month each gaining just over 20% of the vote). What they were reading (again, they could indicate more than one choice) proved interesting, with almost 80% reporting online content (websites, blogs); magazines were second at 60% (*Archaeology, Current World Archaeology,* and *National Geographic* received frequent mention). Archaeological and historical fiction was also prominently represented.

Asking people to identify a favorite book or article was badly received in many quarters, given the impossibility of choosing "just one." Where people did opine, Egypt proved a popular thread, from publications about

King Tut, to Elizabeth Peters's Amelia Peabody mysteries, to the memoir of Joseph Lindon Smith, *Tombs, Temples, and Ancient Art* (1956). Some popular warhorses – C. W. Ceram's *Gods, Graves and Scholars* (first published in 1951 and still in print today, the German original having first appeared in 1949), James Michener's *The Source* (1965), James Deetz's, *In Small Things Forgotten* (1977) – were named, and are also to be found among the choices of the well-known archaeological writers interviewed in Chapter 11. Conversely, the works of some of those same writers, such as Brian Fagan and Colin Renfrew, also appear on the list. Newer offerings too made the cut, such as the fictional accounts written to convey archaeological theory and method (Adrian Praetzellis's *Death by Theory* [2003] and *Dug to Death* [2011]), and Craig Childs's *Finders Keepers: A Tale of Archaeological Plunder and Obsession* [2010]).

Whatever the medium of communication, it is worth observing that current archaeological news (at the time of writing, for example, the reburial of Richard III in Leicester, following the archaeological discovery and analysis of his physical remains) generates significant, if usually short-lived, waves of curiosity, providing a transitory space in which to capture interest and to provide additional channels to explore. One obvious way to collect attention on the fly, of course, is through social media. Almost 60% of the respondents use Facebook as a means to follow archaeological news and share thoughts; Twitter, Academia.edu, and other platforms (Pinterest, GooglePlus) also made an appearance. The ADLS Facebook page itself (largely curated by Dufton) boasts over 7,000 "likes," and in 2015 our posts reached on average over 2,000 people, with c. 10% of those actively sharing posts or clicking through to read linked articles.

What is interesting is that, despite this social media savvy, 81% of individuals said they did not follow a particular archaeologist online. There are exceptions (e.g., Paul Blinkhorn of TimeTeam, or UCLA's Kara Cooney). Yet even with Cooney and TimeTeam hitting over 50,000 Facebook "likes," this remains in marked contrast to, for example, the reach and impact of astrophysicist Neil deGrasse Tyson, with his 3.4 million followers. There appear to be two models at work here: people who value and follow a recognizable and appealing subject online, versus those drawn to a less immediately familiar or attractive discipline by a charismatic individual.

Given the high degree of online curiosity manifested in these survey results, we would argue that archaeology's relative lack of a popular figure or figures to catalyze attention is one opportunity missed. An additional observation in support of this point is the resounding 90% who rated the importance and efficacy of media other than printed texts (e.g., videos, pictures, audio, etc.) for spreading the word about archaeology as Very

Important (63%) or Somewhat Important (27%). In terms of the biggest return on investment, therefore, what would appear most sensible and forward-looking – and what the people appear to want – is the provision of quality material widely and freely available online, and of strengthening ways to point people in the right direction. Online dissemination also facilitates the inclusion of the alternative media mentioned above, freed from some of the practical limitations of printed publications. Sites such as *TrowelBlazers: Women in Archaeology, Geology and Paleontology*, the *Day of Archaeology*, or *Chasing Aphrodite: The Hunt for Looted Antiquities in the World's Museums* come to mind as particularly positive examples contributing original content, as do reliable news sources such as *Heritage Daily* or *Archaeology* magazine.

Patterns in Active Engagement

The necessity of finding flexible and "long-distance" means of communicating archaeology is also underscored by our query about the frequency with which people visit sites or museums. Less than once a month (65%) was the majority report, with 2–3 times a month a distant second (19%), and only a few reporting visits more often than that. As for actual hands-on involvement in field or museum volunteering, the "Nos" had it at 73%. More encouragingly, the 700 or so individuals who answered "Yes" provided a broad-spectrum list of places and activities. Countries included Kenya, Mexico, Bulgaria, Australia, Israel, Canada, Spain, India, Slovenia and more, as well as the United States and United Kingdom. Museum volunteering was also popular, for example at the Detroit Institute of Arts, the Museum of Byzantine Culture in Thessaloniki, the Florence Nightingale Museum in London, the National Museum in New Delhi, and the Museum of Archaeology and Ethnology of the University of São Paulo, Brazil. Specific activities included washing pottery shreds [*sic*] and labeling at Rathfarnham Castle in Dublin, writing grants for Civil War site preservation efforts, or participating in various Archaeology Day (or Week, or Month) activities around the world.

As for the question "if not, why not involved?", some of the answers (of which people could select more than one) were relatively predictable, such as time restrictions (51%) and family commitments (23%). Expectable but unfortunate was the 27% who noted financial restrictions. Not listed as options, but frequent among the more specific comments, were age and health ("I don't like bending"), and to a lesser extent geographic distance from opportunities, either on-site or in museums. A few murmurs were also heard about believing volunteers were not welcome, which can indeed be the case, either because of national regulations or because – and fairly – taking on volunteer labor can be a genuine burden for projects that are not carefully organized to do so.

The chief reason named for discouraging active participation, however, was that of not knowing about available opportunities (59%). Information flow again proves the problem, and thus one that would benefit from more directed and higher visibility online interventions, specifically targeting freely and widely available platforms. Straightforward field schools, usually for credit and with fees, have established listing services (for example, through the Archaeological Institute of America or Shovelbums), but these are probably not the type of opportunity the majority of our sample population seeks. Opportunities for volunteering can be found, as many of the responses received indicate: there are numerous projects that welcome "amateurs" out there, but locating and being near them is the trick.

It is vital to underscore that fieldwork is far from the only possibility; local museums and historical societies, state archaeological offices, and libraries could equally provide space for the interested. One positive way forward would be finding ways to mediate between individuals and opportunities, to match-make location, time commitment, skills required, and so on. Offering some kind of training, perhaps at least in part online, to prepare volunteers for basic tasks could also offset the time investment otherwise required of often already chronically busy professionals. Finally, crowd-sourcing is becoming a feasible way to assist archaeological and museum projects from the comfort of your own home: there are initiatives supported by, among others, the Institute of Archaeology at University College London, the British Museum, and the University of Pennsylvania Museum. Our conclusion, to sum up, is that there are many motivated individuals out there who just don't know how to help.

Patterns in perceptions of the archaeological future

To close the survey, we asked our audience a series of questions about the future. What are the biggest threats to our shared cultural heritage? Who do we study when we study the past? And why should we care about archaeology as a discipline? Starting with the negative side of things, our sample population was asked to rank the severity of six major threats to worldwide heritage, from most (1) to least (6) concerning.

Looting/vandalism and armed conflict landed, unsurprisingly, at the top of the list. 27% of the respondents selected looting/vandalism as their top choice, while 26.5% named armed conflict; so the two taken together were identified as the most worrying threat by more than half of our responding participants. Given the unstable political climate across much of the Middle East at the time of writing, and the significance of the performance of heritage destruction to the wider propaganda of the so-called Islamic State, the loss of archaeological resources is front-and-center in the media and, it would seem, the public consciousness.

The second tier of perceived threat was comprised of the impacts of development and environmental degradation, and the lack of funding for cultural heritage. We had, *prima facie*, expected that media attention to global warming and sea-level changes would have stimulated more substantial indications of environment concern, but it may be that the danger they pose to cultural heritage – despite attention from organizations such as UNESCO's World Heritage Centre – remains under-appreciated. Heritage funding proved to be the option with least consensus. The responses were almost equally divided among the six ranks, indicating that the number of people who believe funding shortages to be the most important threat to cultural heritage is roughly equal to the number who think it is the least important. While opinions likely reflect national, regional, or socio-economic experience, their variety also raises questions about the general degree of understanding about heritage costs and heritage support.

Coming clearly last for our audience were the negative effects of tourist traffic on archaeological sites. This too was somewhat surprising: the impact of tourists at sites such as Pompeii and Petra featured heavily in the ADLS materials, and was an extremely popular topic for discussion in the course's online discussion forums. But directed and memorable media attention to conflict and destruction seems to have carried the day on this topic.

The question – "are you interested in archaeology to find out something about yourself and your past, or to learn about the past of somebody else?" – posed to encourage free text responses, received numerous one-word answers of "Yes" (and a few of "No"). While some people did point to specific cultures of interest (the Maya, ancient Greece, Neanderthals, Armenia), the overwhelming majority indicated that they saw this as a false dichotomy, saying either "Both" or something akin to "Everybody's past". This reaction linked directly to responses to the final question, why anyone should care about archaeology, represented here in Word Cloud form on p. 129.

The same question was asked on the questionnaire sent to authors in Ch. 11 – and comparing the answers is interesting. Resonances exist between Renfrew's "There is no doubt that everyone should care about archaeology. For it answers one of the great questions: Who are We? It does so by revealing how we came to be what we have become" (on p. 160) and a survey participant quoting Marcus Garvey, "A people without the knowledge of their past history, origin, and culture is like a tree without roots"; or betweeen Fagan's "Archaeology is the only way we have of studying human societies over immensely long periods of time and our complex, ever changing adaptations to global environments and to climate change" (on p. 161) and another anonymous contributor's "Because it tells us something about how our species has adapted to past challenges, and because it's wicked cool."

Other threads in the commentary raised issues of conservation and responsibility for cultural heritage ("once it's lost, it's lost forever"), and a strong emphasis on the past's ability to reify our common humanity ("It is the place we all have come from"; "Perhaps if we can understand where we came from we'd have an easier time understanding each other"; "It's our history! The history of mankind!"). In some cases, archaeology's ability to expand our understanding of the past beyond dominant, usually textually-based narratives was cited.

What largely governed the responses to our questionnaire, however, was a fairly instrumentalist view of the field, with numerous paraphrasings of George Santayana's dictum, "Those who cannot remember the past are condemned to repeat it" or Edmund Burke's "People will not look forward to posterity, who never look backward to their ancestors." This is, of course, a commonplace when we talk about the past and, at first blush, it is difficult either to disagree or to argue. Yet what this heartfelt and cheering faith in archaeology reveals is a belief that archaeology always tells the truth about the past, always clarifies rights and wrongs, and always provides sound counsel for the future.

Archaeology's long-term perspective undoubtedly provides valuable insight into patterns of success, failure, and adaptation over the millennia; recent efforts have been made to learn from or even resuscitate specific ancient practices or technologies (such as hydraulic management) in belated realization of lessons to be learned (e.g., Salameh 2004; Spencer 2000). Nor would we ever deny, or want to deny, archaeology's seemingly effortless ability to entrance and enlighten so very many, so very different people. Yet the histories and complexities of the field must equally be acknowledged: that what archaeologists and their consumers make of, and do with, the material past is not in all cases beneficent and balanced.

In the end, what emerged for us as chief lessons for an Archaeology of the People is to reach people young (but never give up trying), and to create flexible, accessible, and quality resources (especially online) with which they might engage. Other activities can follow from that good beginning. For us, the chief joys of an Archaeology for the People proved an affirming passion for the past and, in our sample at least, an optimism for the future; as one individual put it, "the more we understand, the more we can free ourselves of the past and create a better world." Conversely, one clear challenge is how to embolden a thoughtful critique of Archaeology, by the People, and instilling an appreciation that any understanding of the past is an ever-moving target. It is our hope that the strength of the former will allow the necessity of the latter.

Responses to the *Archaeology for the People* Questionnaire

KARA COONEY, BRIAN FAGAN, ALFREDO GONZÁLEZ-RUIBAL,
YANNIS HAMILAKIS, CORNELIUS HOLTORF, MARILYN
JOHNSON, LEONARDO LÓPEZ LUJÁN, AND COLIN RENFREW

Question 1:

What is your favorite book or article about archaeology that is accessible to a non-specialized audience? Why?

Brian Fagan: I don't really have a favorite, for there are very few books or articles that are free of the increasingly specialized scholarship of archaeology. At a serious level, I think that Cyprian Broodbank's *The Making of the Middle Sea* (2013) is a lovely, beautifully written essay that is truly multidisciplinary. At a more popular compass, Francis Pryor's books like *Britain B.C.* (2003) and *Britain A.D.* (2004) are wonderfully conversational, yet written by a really good archaeologist. They have, of course, a UK and European slant. I hate to say this, but Jared Diamond's books, although provocative, are not well written and are often downright turgid. There are, of course, numerous other titles, but these are just suggestions. I think anyone contemplating popular archaeology writing should peruse issues of *Archaeology* magazine and *Current Archaeology*.

Colin Renfrew: My favorite book about archaeology remains *Gods, Graves and Scholars*, by C. W. Ceram, first published in 1949, and still in print. I understand that it has sold five million copies. I read it shortly after it was published and it seemed then, and still does, to conjure up the romance of archaeology.

Alfredo González-Ruibal: Without a doubt, James Deetz's *In Small Things Forgotten* (1977). He managed to write a text that is thought-provoking, empirically rich and sophisticated, and at the same time accessible to the wider public (as proved by his 512 ratings and 34 reviews in goodreads.com), thanks to its clarity and literary style. One can say that it is easier to craft an interesting story doing historical archaeology rather than prehistoric. There is a truth to it. But what is remarkable about this book is that, unlike a lot of historical archaeology, the narrative is guided by artifacts, not by texts. It is pure archaeology and immensely readable.

Marilyn Johnson: I was very taken with the short book *In Small Things Forgotten* by James Deetz and have returned to it several times. It manages to be both evocative and informative, and in its small, focused, particular way, reminds us that archaeology fills in the story of the lives that didn't make it into the history books. But is it my favorite? It is more male-centric than I like, but I have a shelf of wonderful counterweights that includes *The Invisible Sex* by Adovasio, Soffer, and Page (2007) and Sarah Milledge Nelson's *Gender in Archaeology* (1997).

I don't quite know how Charles C. Mann wrote *1491: New Revelations of the Americas before Columbus* (2005), but I was so enthralled, I tracked him down. I tore out his chapter about cotton (or anchovies) and maize, and traveled to Peru with it in my pocket. I also enjoyed *Turn Right at Machu Picchu* by Mark Adams (2011), Heather Pringle's *The Mummy Congress* (2001), and David Grann's terrific *The Lost City of Z* (2009).

I'd be remiss if I didn't add that all of the people in my book, *Lives in Ruins* (2014), are communicators, excellent at explaining (often colorfully) what they are doing and, in their own writing, engaging on the page (Sarah Nelson is a good example). I don't think I could have penetrated the intersection of the military and archaeology, for instance, without Laurie Rush's lively voice, or become excited about the classics without Joan Breton Connelly's writing, or understood anything about Paleolithic archaeology without John Shea's.

Cornelius Holtorf: David Macauley's *Motel of the Mysteries* (1979) is a classic parody of archaeology. It gives people, old and young, a big smile on their face when they think about the business that archaeologists are engaged in. Another favorite, making me smile a lot on the inside, is Gregory Benford's *Deep Time* (1999). Benford presents a fascinating discussion of some bold archaeological questions that are normally associated with other realms.

Leonardo López Luján: I very much enjoy all the books in the "Digging for the Past" series which was edited by Brian Fagan for Oxford University Press. These are books aimed at young adults interested in the great civilizations of antiquity. Their main advantages include their affordable price, small format, and also that they are hardcover books that are well-designed and profusely illustrated. As for their content, this series gets it right in offering texts that have been written both by a professional archaeologist whose research concerns the book's main topic and by an author who specializes in writing for children and young adults. This results in books that are well written and contain information that is correct and up-to-date.

Kara Cooney: I would say that the Elizabeth Peters series is the best non-specialized introduction to archaeology and Egyptology, my own field. They are fiction, of course, but they were written by Barbara Mertz, who received her Ph.D. in Egyptology from the Oriental Institute at the University of Chicago. She gets her facts – about 19th-century dig methods, about Egyptian gods and goddesses, about sites – right. The non-specialist learns about archaeology without even being aware of it.

Yannis Hamilakis: David Lowenthal's *The Past is a Foreign Country* (1985), due to come out in a revised edition in 2015. Not strictly "archaeology," but central to the nature and operation of the discipline. It foregrounds the role of material heritage in the contemporary moment, addressing at the same time a range of crucial issues, from politics and nationalism to theoretical matters on temporality (discussed under the theme of "creative anachronism"). And all this in a writing style which is accessible to the non-specialist public. The rich illustration content of the book, of course, contributed significantly to its success.

Question 2:

Evolutionary biology, astronomy, geology, biology, oncology, and other hard sciences have had distinguished and successful popularizers (including, for example, Stephen Jay Gould, Carl Sagan, Martin Rudwick, Lewis Thomas, and Siddhartha Mukerjee). Has archaeology had similar specialists who have been capable of reaching and capturing large audiences? If so, who are they, and how do they do it? If not, why not?

Yannis Hamilakis: There were some prominent names in the past, but I do not think that archaeology has such figures today, although there are some successful cases in Classics, and one or two in anthropology (such as David Graeber, for example). Several archaeologists, of course, have produced popular and semi-popular books, and some of them are successful, at least in terms of sales. But have they changed the dominant public perception of the discipline? Have they managed to inform public opinion and public policy on the fundamental and urgent matters of our time, such as climate change, war and militarisation, global migration from the developing world, poverty and inequality, debt and neo-colonialism?

The reasons for such absence are many and diverse. Popular writing and communication with the public are not technical matters, are not to do with a "right formula" which, if found, will guarantee success. They are linked directly to our perception of the discipline and its ontological status. In other words, the scholarly, academic understanding of archaeology shapes the archaeologists' attempts to go beyond their peers, and reach the wider public sphere. I have argued, time and again, that a fundamental ethical-cum-ontological problem for today's archaeology is its restrictive modernist heritage, its professionalization, its self-guarding and policing of its boundaries (seen as essential in reasserting its autonomy vis-à-vis history, classics, and anthropology), its self-definition as a discipline of the past, the main ethical responsibility of which is the stewardship, preservation, and interpretation of the entity which it calls "the archaeological record" (e.g., Hamilakis 2007). It is no coincidence that, in the past, some of the most successful archaeological popularisers were not strictly professional in our contemporary sense: they had a wider education and sensibility, and had often followed diverse career paths. Our contemporary professionalized approach may have produced some short-term gains, but it is no longer adequate, being at the same time self-serving, and epistemologically as well as ethically and politically problematic and unsustainable. Moreover, the re-emergence of often uncritical and un-theorized science discourses has facilitated the dominance of geneticists and neuroscientists, who seem almost to monopolise the public debates on cultural and social identity and on human experience.

Before we attempt to reach the various publics, thus, we should re-invent archaeology as a contemporary mnemonic practice, a form of cultural production that deals with all material traces from various times, which may inhabit the present but which are, by definition, multi-temporal. This will be a discipline of the present, without being presentist. It will evoke and re-enact various times, also showing their implications and effects on the present and future.

Kara Cooney: I would put Brian Fagan on the list, although he doesn't have a larger media presence. His books are readable, interesting, and well known. I myself tried to create a comparative archaeology/anthropology series with "Out of Egypt," which I co-produced, but I was told by executives at the Discovery Channel that it was "too educational." I am not interested in doing TV work any longer, unless I am also a producer and in control of the content: I have been mis-edited too many times by the History or Discovery Channel to say something I didn't really say. This means that PBS is our only outlet, which is sad, because with government cuts, PBS has become more like the Home Shopping Network than what it was in Carl Sagan's day. Until the media creates more niche outlets, or until we archaeologists can produce directly for an outlet like Netflix, I think the "educational" cable networks will continue to choose cheap and easy reality television, over content led by actual scholars and scientists. Having said all of that, I think Jared Diamond is the closest mass-popularizer archaeology has, and he is a geographer...

Although not an archaeologist, Bill Nye is also an interesting case, because to create his media presence he essentially had to leave the field and move into media full-time. Such choices are real, and I know them intimately. It is very difficult for a university professor to engage in media work on the side. There are only so many hours in the day...

Colin Renfrew: Archaeology has had its best-sellers: *Nineveh and its Remains* by A. H. Layard was one of the first, in 1848. Sir Mortimer Wheeler's *Archaeology from the Earth* did well enough in 1954. In our own day some of Brian Fagan's books have done rather well. But sadly none has recently rivalled in sales such pseudo-science as Erich von Daniken's *Chariots of the Gods*, first published in 1968. I suspect that one reason is that the best archaeologists find actually doing archaeology more exciting and interesting than writing general books about it.

Marilyn Johnson: I like David Hurst Thomas, and he's distinguished and popular. I know Ian Tattersall and Chris Stringer are both distinguished and popular. Bill Bryson, though – wouldn't it be fun if he did a whole book on an archaeological subject?

Cornelius Holtorf: It is all a matter of good story-telling. I think Archaeology has its share of great story-tellers. Two Germans in that category were C. W. Ceram and Rudolf Pörtner. Today, archaeological stories regularly reach large audiences in many countries without necessarily depending on single individuals.

Brian Fagan: I really don't follow who is doing this. I think that the only people who effectively write full time for the public in archaeology are Paul Bahn and I. Our expertises are very different. There are others, who are more on the scholarly side, such as Chris Scarre or David Lewis-Williams, the rock art expert. Thames and Hudson seems to have the most success with popular archaeology writings, although they tend to be on the more specialized side. But they seem to be cutting back the number of archaeology titles they publish. (I think everyone is.) The narrow publish-or-perish syndrome which infects archaeology and a still persistent belief that popular writing is lightweight and not scholarly still pervade much of archaeology, and indeed, anthropology.

Alfredo González-Ruibal: I would like to mention a Spanish case here: the Atapuerca research team. Atapuerca is one of the most important palaeolithic sites in Eurasia for understanding the evolution of human beings. The co-directors of the research, Juan Luis Arsuaga, Eudald Carbonell, and José María Bermúdez de Castro, have not only published high-impact articles which have revolutionized our knowledge of human evolution, they have also published books that have been exceedingly popular in Spain (e.g. Arsuaga and Martínez 2004). In fact, Spaniards no longer associate archaeology with mummies or dinosaurs, but with the Palaeolithic (which is a problem for those of us who work on the opposite end of human evolution!). The directors of the Atapuerca project are considerably more famous than most other scientific popularizers in the country. However, part of their success lies in the fact that their research is situated at the intersection between the natural sciences and archaeology: Arsuaga himself, the most visible head, is a geologist. I would not say, therefore, that their success can be explained uniquely by them being savvy popularizers (which they are). Still, what has made their work fascinating for the public has been their storytelling ability: they have been able to produce a relevant narrative using things (basically, bones of people and animals and lithic tools). Any archaeologist should be able to do that. However, the narrative of human origins is difficult to match.

Of course, we always have the archaeo-appeal, as Cornelius Holtorf (2005) has pointed out, but we should also be wary of its dangers: astrophysicists do not have to resort to aliens, or biologists to monsters, in order to make their discipline attractive to the wider public (even if those are enrolled regularly). Perhaps we should emphasize more the relevance of archaeology as a mode of intellectual production, something that might be exciting because it addresses big questions that have an impact in the present, as Michael Shanks has noted (http://documents.stanford.edu/michaelshanks/61?view=print). In fact, there are some archaeologists that are following this path, like Ian Morris (2010) and David Wengrow (2010). To a large extent, this path was opened by people like Bill Rathje decades before: his main concern was showing the relevance of archaeology in addressing big contemporary issues, from garbage management to ecological crises (e.g., Rathje and Murphy 1992). For me, this is one of the ways archaeology can become simultaneously more popular and more relevant. This does not mean that we have to forget about the archaeo-appeal, but rather that we have to convince people that exciting discoveries and archaeological adventures are all the more interesting when they allow us to reflect on relevant issues for the fate of humanity, past and present.

Leonardo López Luján: Without a doubt, the best writer in our field in terms of outreach is the archaeologist Brian Fagan. He has published dozens of books for the greater public, all of which have been successful commercially. Fagan is a distinguished specialist who has been able to translate the technical language of our discipline into knowledge that is easy to understand by the greater public. He has the double virtue of being a protagonist in our field, and, at the same time, a master of the essential tools required to transmit his knowledge in written and oral form.

Question 3:

The astrophysicist Neil deGrasse Tyson has over two million likes on Facebook – much more by several factors than any archaeologist we know of. Is there something about archaeology that inherently eludes the radical reductions demanded by social media? What other factors might be involved?

Marilyn Johnson: I don't begrudge Tyson his Facebook likes, and I think his popularity has less to do with the fact that he's an astrophysicist than with his personality. He is a charismatic scientist and his reach is good for everyone in the sciences. (And, just between us, I think "the radical reductions demanded by social media" dooms that question.) People who can capture the popular imagination are unusual and they pop up where they will.

Leonardo López Luján: I do not think that astrophysics and archaeology are fundamentally different. Such differences must be due to other causes. One of these could be that archaeology students take classes in universities in which students are not taught to engage in outreach that is also of high technical quality.

Kara Cooney: I don't think so. My own Facebook page is approaching 60,000 "likes," and I have no TV show. Tyson has a weekly TV show. If one of us had such a platform, this would be possible.

  Also – I think we can make a go at popularizing, with the understanding that it will always be niche in comparison to the big hitters from astrophysics and biological sciences. Archaeology is, and always will be, a smaller thing than the "science" that Carl Sagan or Neil deGrasse Tyson represent. A quick look at the grant dollars from the US Government is illustrative of this. Given that we are a smaller group of scientists, I also suspect that popularizers in our field do feel more of a personal sting from their colleagues who might push back at what you call "radical reductions."

Colin Renfrew: Archaeology is like history in the sense that it is a long story with many fascinating and crucial moments, occurring in different parts of the world. It cannot successfully be encapsulated in focusing on just one grand discovery at one time and place.

Brian Fagan: I do not work with social media, which would consume far too much of my time. But I suspect that archaeology does not have the spectacular appeal of much of astronomy or, indeed history. It usually comes down to early fossils, royal burials, hoards, and pyramids. The success of *Time Team* in the UK has been truly remarkable, but there is a long tradition of popular archaeology in Britain that is not found here in the USA, where so much archaeology is the history of "them" and not of "us." It is no coincidence that the most popular topics here are the Ancient Maya and the Inca, as well as South American mummies. They fit the popular image of archaeology. There is no archaeologist that I know of who has a wide popular following – but this may be because archaeology is not a very glamorous TV subject.

Alfredo González-Ruibal: I have the feeling that archaeology is still not regarded as a respectable science in the way astrophysics or evolutionary biology are. It is considered to be somewhat in the fringe: the image of the archaeologists is too much associated with mummies and mysterious ruins. While this admittedly attracts a lot of followers, it also keeps at bay many others who are interested in the "serious" (i.e. natural) sciences that can solve big problems. In my opinion, the questions addressed by astrophysicists and biologists are not necessarily more amenable to the Internet format than archaeological questions. One can tackle rather complex issues online. In my own experience – I run a collective blog on the archaeology of the Spanish Civil War (http://guerraenlauniversidad.blogspot.com.es) – when my colleagues or I write entries that have to do with the political, social or even epistemological aspects of archaeology, the posts receive more visits than those that describe sites or finds (even spectacular finds).

For me, the main difference between post-Palaeolithic archaeology and the other sciences is that archaeology is always local. Galaxies are universal and so are the Pliocene and the Australopithecines, since we all come from them. It does not matter if you are from Hungary or Canada: brown dwarfs affect you (or don't) the same. However, if you are from Hungary you will probably be more interested in the history of the Huns than in the Inuit. It does not matter how wide and ambitious are the anthropological questions behind our research: it will still attract a larger local, national or even continental audience (as opposed to global). One continental example: whereas pre-Columbian archaeology features prominently in popular archaeology in the United States, it receives a relatively small share of interest in Europe, where the Romans, the Greeks and the Celts occupy much more space in archaeology magazines, TV programs and social media. This has a lot to do with identity, of course. Where I come from, people discuss hotly on the Internet whether they are Celts or just Gallaecians and this goes hand in hand with an interest in Iron Age hill forts. A similar debate would not make sense in astrophysics and very little in geology or biology (even if one may develop an interest for species or geological formations in the neighborhood). Again, those works that have archaeological references and at the same time have managed to attract a large and global audience deal with global issues: Jared Diamond or Ian Morris. An internet post or a tweet on Bronze Age Crete will have a hard time to become viral at a global level. The discovery of an exo-planet has it much easier.

Yannis Hamilakis: Many archaeologists use social media today, but as I have tried to show above, being in the social media does not offer the magic solution; it will not make archaeology automatically "cool" and accessible. My presence on Facebook and Twitter have brought me in contact with many non-specialists, but most of these people are normally indifferent to many of the issues we call strictly "archaeological." They are, however, very interested in learning how archaeology can help us understand the important social and political matters of the present. Some of the most widely read pieces I have produced are to do with the present-day political implications of archaeological knowledge, and of archaeological monuments and sites. Stories about the material past itself, of course, can be fascinating and of wider interest. But let's remember that every present-day perception of the material past, scholarly or other, is full of memories, is mediated by contemporary mnemonic recollections and experiences. It is also mediated by affective impulses, from nostalgia, to the desire for radical alterity, for other, better worlds, be they in the deep past or in other galaxies. Demonstrating the material and temporal nature of experience and at the same time foregrounding historical contingency, showing that things could have been otherwise, against all forms of teleological thinking, are some of the most important things we could do as archaeologists.

Cornelius Holtorf: There is no reason why archaeologists should not be as successful and likeable on Facebook and in other social media as they are as characters in Hollywood films, in computer games or in literature. But archaeology remains a little discipline, although one that is known by many.

Question 4:

After we launched the Archaeology for the People contest, several potential participants criticized us for accepting only written articles (as opposed to opening up the contest to, say, photography, video, comic-strips, and web-based pieces such as podcasts and blogs). How important and effective do you think media other than printed texts are in the dissemination of archaeological information to non-specialized audiences? Have you yourself used such 'alternative' media?

Cornelius Holtorf: Moving images are of particular importance for reaching large audiences today: they can convey carefully defined messages more easily and in a more memorable way than texts. I do not see myself as a popularizer of archaeology, but I once commissioned a conference publication in the form of a graphic novel (*Places, People, Stories*, 2012) and facilitated recording of archaeological lectures and debates on film.

Alfredo González-Ruibal: I am all for old printed media when it comes to producing academic works. And when I say old media, I really mean it: I think we could produce books with watercolors and engravings as the antiquarians of two hundred years ago did (if anybody would be interested in publishing such kind of things). When one sees nineteenth-century archaeological reports, such as the publication of the German excavations at Olympia, one has the feeling that we have lost something. Video and digital imagery are not all. At the same time, I am aware that new media are extremely important to reach wider audiences, more than paper-based publications, and they allow us to play with older media, as well. The blog and a Facebook page of my Spanish Civil War archaeology project are quite popular, at least in relative terms: we have almost 7,000 followers on Facebook (https://www.facebook.com/arqueologia.delaguerracivilespanola.9), which might sound ridiculous, but it is not bad for a page in Spanish dealing with a very specialized project and an unusual kind of archaeology. Our blog has received half a million hits since 2009. Also, the Internet provides a public forum which is unavailable with more traditional forms of dissemination. We have received many comments, many of them quite brutal and outrageous, but these are perhaps the most useful, because they allow us to understand deep sociological issues that do not emerge in the polite world of public lectures, guided tours and exhibitions. One can learn a lot from insults.

Brian Fagan: What your participants are criticizing the editors for is nonsense. Yes, the visual is important, as are blogs, but the issue here is properly written, engaging essays on archaeology. And certainly these other media do not encourage literacy – often quite the contrary. One of the biggest problems in archaeology, apart from a lot of it being unspectacular and frankly dull, is that very few archaeologists are trained to be good writers for general audiences. What these folk are proposing is a cop-out – and, I suspect, in some cases, an unwillingness to put the work in. Yes, other media than text are important, *if* they are done really well. I have used many alternative media, including TV and film, also radio and multimedia course formats. In my view, one of the most effective ways of communicating to wider audiences is through radio. It is short, to the point – and people listen to it in their cars. Having said all this, I think material developed for the iPad and phones would be very effective *if* the subject matter engages people from the beginning. Do you do this by using first person experience, evocative reconstructions, or just vivid writing? They all can work, but so much depends on the subject matter. For what it's also worth, I think that really good, well-illustrated lectures are very powerful – and underrated. I suspect that down the line we are going to see superb multi-media interactive books on the Web, but the expense of doing them, especially getting permission for images, is inhibiting development.

Colin Renfrew: The most popular medium for archaeology so far has been television. Indeed in the UK *Animal, Vegetable, Mineral* made Sir Mortimer Wheeler and then Glyn Daniel TV Personality of the Year in successive years. The transmission time taken up by archaeology exceeds that of nearly every other field, at least in the UK, although David Attenborough's programs on wild life have led the field in recent years.

Since you ask for personal reminiscence, my own BBC-TV Chronicle programs *The Tree that Put the Clock Back* and *Islands Out of Time* had good viewing figures in their day, and *Lost Kings of the Desert* gave a fair impression of Hatra, now reportedly destroyed by the so-called Islamic State. Today the programs on the archaeology of Central and South America by the British Museum's Jago Cooper are popular and authoritative, although they do not yet outshine Attenborough.

Leonardo López Luján: I have been involved in various projects that have attempted to disseminate archaeological knowledge on a large scale, including blogs, podcasts, videos, and video-games. All of these are high impact and effective, inasmuch as they offer information at a global scale and almost always in forms that are immediate and at no cost. Nevertheless, I am confident that none of them can supersede the power, authority, and precision of the written word, as it appears in articles published in highly prestigious outreach magazines

Marilyn Johnson: I absolutely relied on a variety of websites and alternate media sources to research my book about archaeologists. I was influenced by Trent de Boer's *Shovel Bum: Comix of Archaeological Field Life* (2004) and (among others) by Naked Archaeology and the Archaeology Channel's podcasts; DigVentures's Twitter feed; the Smithsonian's website and Texas A & M's website for the Center for the Study of the First Americans; Bill Caraher's wonderful blog Archaeology of the Mediterranean World, and the illuminating TrowelBlazers blog; and one of my favorite sources for archaeological knowledge, Archaeology's Dirty Little Secrets, Sue Alcock and the Joukowsky Institute's course on Coursera.

Yannis Hamilakis: If archaeology is a contemporary mnemonic practice and cultural production at the same time, then it goes without saying that *all* artistic, performative, and literary media share with archaeology certain affinities, and all should be available for us to experiment with. They are extremely important in communicating with non-specialist audiences, and at the same time they can evoke the multi-sensorial and affective nature of materiality and temporality, and of archaeological work. I have extensively used various such media myself, in collaboration with colleagues and creative artists: from photo-essays (e.g., Hamilakis and Ifantidis 2013) and photo-ethnographic blogging (www.kalaureiainthepresent.org), to semi-literary writing in academic publications and books (e.g., Hamilakis 2013), to theater-archaeology experiments (e.g., Hamilakis and Theou 2013), often as part of the shared, creative space that archaeological ethnography can engender. Such theater-archaeology performances were attended by hundreds of people in the rural countryside, as well as in Athenian restaurants and other venues. In a recent work, I experiment with a combination of poetic writing and photography, attempting to evoke the contemporary Athenian crisis-scape through an archaeological sensibility (Hamilakis 2015). Several of these publications appear in scholarly fora, but all of them are also disseminated in social media, whereas some others have accompanying photo-blogs (www.theotheracropolis.com).

Kara Cooney: I think it's very important to use non-written media. Everyone I know, including myself, has just too much to read. There is *always* a stack of things to read. Any means of communicating information that moves outside formal "reading" would be appreciated and create a freshness, a seduction.

For example, I am working on a coffins database right now, trying quickly and clearly to communicate complicated wood-panel painted scenes from the 21st Dynasty. With multiple levels of tagging on the visual medium and hopefully with some 3D photography, I will be able to abandon the deadly boring, unreadable, and unusable thick description most coffin studies have included. I will also be able to compare tagged scenes from coffin to coffin, allowing analysis that written description does not. Archaeology is visual. Are there ways to create visual ciphers that can be quickly consumed and analyzed by our brains? Instead of writing something about stratigraphy, can we create visual codes, even comic books, which combine limited text and extensive and colorful imagery?

Question 5:

For whom do you write?

Brian Fagan: I mainly write books, ranging from long established textbooks for colleges and universities to volumes for National Geographic. Mainline trade houses such as Bloomsbury or Basic Books publish most of my work. (The entire non-fiction writing scene is changing fundamentally, not only because of e-books, but also because of smaller sales of serious non-fiction, a product of gross saturation in the marketplace.)

I have also written popular articles for all manner of outlets from *The Los Angeles Times, The New York Times* and *Wall Street Journal*, to *Gentleman's Quarterly* and *Smithsonian*, as well, of course, as *Archaeology Magazine*. I've also consulted widely for TV and radio series and published two courses with *Great Courses* (formerly known as *The Teaching Company*).

Cornelius Holtorf: Since with most of my work I intend to contribute to academic debate, I write a lot in academic journals and books. My main audiences are thus students and fellow researchers in my own and related disciplines. I also experience pleasure in the writing process as such, and in that sense I write for myself.

Kara Cooney: This depends on what it is. I actually use my formal and legal name Kathlyn M. Cooney for my scholarly writing and Kara Cooney for my popular writing. I don't know if anyone notices, but I do. I know that they are different. If I'm writing about my work on funerary reuse during the

Bronze Age collapse, I write for the specialist. But this same work has been popular among non-specialized audiences, and so I could imagine including that research in some of my popular writing.

For my last book, *The Woman Who Would Be King* (2014), an openly conjectural and personalized biography about Hatshepsut, I wrote for anyone with an interest in people, in power, or in the ancient world. If the narrative was getting bogged down with historiography or scholarly disagreement, that information was moved to an endnote. That way, the scholarly information is still there, but it doesn't pull the story away from the main character and her struggles. As I suspected might happen, the book received a very critical review in *KMT*, an Egyptology magazine, and a very favorable review in *Time*. There is indeed push-back when the scholar experiments with human emotion, whimsy, or conjecture, trying to flesh out characters from the ancient world.

Colin Renfrew: In a sense I write for myself. That is to say I write about what interests me. I have not deliberately contrived to make my books more popular, even when writing for a more general audience, as for instance in *Before Civilization: The Radiocarbon Revolution and Prehistoric Europe* (1973) or in *Archaeology and Language: The Puzzle of Indo-European Origins* (1988). Setting out the argument clearly has seemed the main objective. But perhaps there is a lesson there which I have not yet learnt!

Alfredo González-Ruibal: I write on paper for my peers (I would like to think they are more than archaeologists) and on the Internet for the wider public. It is an excellent exercise, by the way, that informs and shapes my academic writing, so there is a lot of permeability. I have also written a popular book in Spanish on the archaeology of the Spanish Civil War (still waiting a publisher), because new media do not reach everybody (I, for one, read many books and articles and very few blogs and webpages) and because books are still necessary to develop a complex argument. There is also a blurred genre, which is that of field reports: I write my excavation reports in a way that can be satisfactory for the expert (they have all the information: finds catalogues, stratigraphic units, maps) and at the same time can be accessible for the non-specialist. I try not to write reports in an esoteric style that looks very scientific but often makes them difficult to follow even for other archaeologists. My aim is to produce a narrative. After all, to describe the excavation of a site is to tell the story of that site. The reports are uploaded on our institutional digital repository (http://digital.csic.es) and it is mostly the wider public, rather than other archaeologists, that download them. I would also emphasize the importance of talking, especially in countries where people do not read much. Public lectures are very important.

Leonardo López Luján: As any archaeologist does, I produce very different types of publications aimed at diverse audiences. Broadly speaking, I can say, on the one hand, that I write specialized books and articles aimed at my archaeologist colleagues and at professionls in related fields concerned with the study and understanding of the remote past. But on the other hand, I write for the so-called greater public. Since I work at a site-museum (Museo del Templo Mayor; templomayor.inah.gob.mex) I frequently edit catalogues for our temporary shows and these allow visitors to take home with them information additional to what they saw in the museum. I am also actively involved in the journal *Arqueología Mexicana*, which has a run of 60,000 copies that are sold throughout my country, but which also reaches many places abroad. This journal's purpose is to communicate to a non-specialized, but educated public the advances of our discipline in Mexico. Finally, I collaborate with major publishing houses and with professional illustrators, crafting stories, accounts, and narratives for children and young adults about the cultures of Mesoamerica.

Marilyn Johnson: I write for myself, to reach for and work out some idea that I have only a vague notion of, and to get access to a part of my brain that I can't get at otherwise. But I rewrite for my parents and my friends. I want to persuade and amuse and share what I'm learning with them. They are all lively and curious people who find the world a bit baffling these days – with good reason.

Yannis Hamilakis: For anyone who can read. But we do not just write: we also produce material realities, images, performances, installations, various multi-sensorial assemblages. We are thus cultural producers for all people, even for the ones – especially for the ones – who cannot read.

Question 6:

Very briefly (just a few sentences), why should anyone care about archaeology?

Alfredo González-Ruibal: Which other discipline can find history in the latrine beneath your house?

Cornelius Holtorf: I don't think anybody needs to "care" for archaeology in the way you care for something that cannot take care of itself. Archaeology is doing remarkably well even beyond academia. Having said that, archaeology is a field that has the potential to fascinate and engage many audiences, and those who choose to ignore archaeology will do so at their peril.

Colin Renfrew: There is no doubt that everyone should care about archaeology. For it answers one of the great questions: Who are We? It does so by revealing how we came to be what we have become. It can do so from the earliest times of a million and more years ago right down to the final exploration of the unknown world in the eighteenth century A.D., and on through the industrial developments which formed the modern era. Archaeology can also reveal the origins and nature of human diversity: the formation of peoples and of nations. It is successfully tracing the history of technology, and beginning to lead to the deeper understanding of human cognition. And its raw material is unending: the material evidence of the past!

Yannis Hamilakis: The most important first step for reaching various publics is the demonstration of relevance; an impoverished, modernist archaeology that deals exclusively with the past and with the "archaeological record" will continue to be seen as irrelevant. A contemporary archaeology, on the other hand, which shows that all urgent present-day matters are, one or way or another, to do with various configurations of temporality and materiality, and with evocations of material history and memory, can become directly relevant. People should care about archaeology, therefore, not because it can tell some stories about the past they did not know, but because archaeology can show how the experience and perception of materiality and temporality shape every aspect of their lives on earth. They should care because it can help them counter presentist notions, and "end of history" neo-liberal agendas, or what Fredric Jameson has called, the "contemporary imprisonment in the present" (2015: 120), at the same time demonstrating the material historicity of the contemporary moment, and the contingent and temporary and thus unstable nature of the current *status quo*. Finally, they should care because, based on its depth-knowledge of human experience on earth over the past two million years, it can help them imagine and invent new forms of living on earth, of cohabiting with non-human animals in a non-anthropocentric world, and of relating to other beings and to all organic and inorganic matter in a non-instrumental, non-exploitative manner.

Marilyn Johnson: "Haven't all the important archaeological sites already been found?," someone asked me. I think this is a common misperception. I always thought archaeology was fascinating, but a bit musty and arcane: broken pottery and bones, ruins, and dead civilizations. Then I observed archaeologists in action, in the context of their sites, and I saw a vital and pulsing frontier. Archaeologists are searching for signs of life in the past, and what they find often astonishes us.

Leonardo López Luján: Archaeology is of enormous importance in Mexico. Given the exceptional historical continuity of our culture, to practice archaeology in my country involves the reconstruction of the past not only as an abstract endeavor, but as the reconstruction of our own past, of the history of our ancestors, of our parents and grandparents. This helps us understand how our society has changed over the centuries; it helps us understand our current situation, and to plan a future in which we will not repeat mistakes, but will replicate historical successes. In this sense archaeology can act for us as a guide and a source of identity.

Kara Cooney: I work on the Bronze Age collapse. When people who fervently believed in the power of funerary materiality were faced with scarcity of that materiality, did they change their beliefs to match the new economic reality? Absolutely not. Instead, they found alternative ways of getting the funerary materiality, including reuse and theft. This is just one small drop in the bucket of collapse studies. As we move towards the largest environmental collapse the globe has ever experienced, research on human reactions to collapse are absolutely vital. I also work with the 18th Dynasty and the height of spending by the royal palace. This brings up questions of social place, of sustainability, of spending – all very topical to us today, as the 1% consumes more than anyone else. There is every reason to care about archaeology. And non-specialists do care. They are hungry to be taught and to learn. They are hungry for real information, not the "ancient aliens" nonsense. We can complain about ANCIENT ALIENS until we are blue in the face; but until archaeologists support each other in producing good and entertaining content that can compete with such shows, we will never win the stage.

Brian Fagan: Archaeology is the only way we have of studying human societies over immensely long periods of time and our complex, ever-changing adaptations to global environments and to climate change. It is also a unique way of examining emerging human diversity and understanding the ways in which we are similar and different. It is a unique mirror into changing human behavior, which forms our common cultural heritage. In short, archaeology helps provide the context for today's rapidly changing world. Finally, for what it is worth, it has immense value for the rapidly expanding cultural tourism industry (cruise ships, jumbo jets, etc., as well as domestic tourism; the latter is huge, even in places like China and Cambodia).

References

Adams, Mark
    2011 *Turn Right at Machu Picchu: Rediscovering the Lost City One Step at a Time*. Dutton, New York.

Adovasio, J. M., Olga Soffer, and Jake Page
    2007 *The Invisible Sex: Uncovering the True Roles of Women in Prehistory*. Collins, New York.

Alcock, Susan E., J. Andrew Dufton, and Müge Durusu-Tanrıöver
    forthcoming   Massive, Open, Online and Opportunistic: Archaeology's Dirty Little Secrets. *Journal of Social Archaeology*.

Archaeology
    2015 *Archaeology: A Publication of the Archaeological Institute of America*. Online Magazine, http://www.archaeology.org, accessed April 15, 2015.

Archaeological Institute of America
    2014 Alex the Archaeologist. http://www.archaeological.org/blog/17095, accessed April 19, 2015.

Arsuaga, Juan Luis de, and Ignacio Martínez
    2004 *La especie elegida: la larga marcha de la evolución humana*. RBA, Barcelona.

Benford, Gregory
    1999 *Deep Time: How Humanity Communicates Across Millennia*. Avon, New York.

Broodbank, Cyprian
    2013 *The Making of the Middle Sea: A History of the Mediterranean from the Beginning to the Emergence of the Classical World*. Thames & Hudson, London.

Ceram, C. W.
    1951 *Gods, Graves and Scholars*. Translated by S. Wilkins and E. B. Garside. Knopf, New York.

Chasing Aphrodite
    2015 *Chasing Aphrodite: The Hunt for Looted Antiquities in the World's Museums*, Web Page, http://chasingaphrodite.com, accessed April 15, 2015, curated by Jason Felch.

Childs, Craig
    2010 *Finders Keepers: A Tale of Archaeological Plunder and Obsession*. Little, Brown and Company, New York.

Coe, Michael D.
    1992 *Breaking the Maya Code*. Thames & Hudson, New York.

Connah, Graham
    2010 *Writing about Archaeology*. Cambridge University Press, Cambridge.

Cooney, Kara
    2014 *The Woman Who Would Be King*. Crown, New York.

Day of Archaeology

    2015   *Day of Archaeology: Find out what archaeologists really do.* Web page, http://www. dayofarchaeology.com, accessed April 15, 2015.

De Boer, Trent

    2004   *Shovel Bum: Comix of Archaeological Field Life.* Altamira Press, Walnut Creek, California.

Deetz, James

    1977   *In Small Things Forgotten: The Archaeology of Early American Life.* Doubleday, New York.

Deloria Jr, Vine

    1995   *Red Earth, White Lies: Native Americans and the Myth of Scientific Fact.* Scribner, New York.

Derrida, Jacques

    1994   *Specters of Marx: The State of the Debt, the Work of Mourning, and the New International.* Routledge, New York.

Diamond, Jared

    1997   *Guns, Germs, and Steel: The Fates of Human Societies.* W. W. Norton, New York.

Echo-Hawk, Roger C.

    2000   Ancient History in the New World: Integrating Oral Traditions and the Archaeological Record in Deep Time. *American Antiquity* 65(2): 267–290.

Eren, Metin I., Robert J. Paten, Michael J. O'Brien, and David J. Meltzer

    2013   Refuting the Technological Cornerstone of the Ice-Age Atlantic Crossing Hypothesis. *Journal of Archaeological Science* 40(7): 2934–2941.

Fagan, Brian

    2006   *Writing Archaeology: Telling Stories about the Past.* Left Coast Press, Walnut Creek, CA.

Gibbon, Edward

    1776–89 [1932]   *The Decline and Fall of the Roman Empire.* The Modern Library, New York.

Gibbons, Ann

    2006   *The First Human: The Race to Discover our Earliest Ancestors.* Doubleday, New York.

Gould, Stephen J.

    1983   *Hen's Teeth and Horses Toes.* Norton, New York.

    1985   *The Flamingo's Smile: Reflections in Natural History.* Norton, New York.

    1991   *Bully for Brontosaurus: Reflections in Natural History.* Norton, New York.

    1998   *Leonardo's Mountain of Clams and the Diet of Worms: Essays on Natural History.* Harmony Books, New York.

Gould, Stephen J., and Richard C. Lewontin

    1979   The Spandrels of San Marco and the Panglossian Paradigm: A Critique of the Adaptationist Programme. *Proceedings of the Royal Society of London* B 205: 581–598.

Grann, David

    2009   *The Lost City of Z: A Tale of Deadly Obsession in the Amazon.* Doubleday, New York.

Hamilakis, Yannis

    2007   From Ethics to Politics. In *Archaeology and Capitalism: From Ethics to Politics,* edited by Yannis Hamilakis and Philip Duke, pp. 15–40. Left Coast Press, Walnut Creek, California.

2013 *Archaeology and the Senses: Human Experience, Memory, and Affect.* Cambridge University Press, Cambridge.

2015 An Athenian, Nocturnal Archaeology (A Photo-Poetic Essay). *Journal of Contemporary Archaeology* 2(1): 149–168.

Hamilakis, Yannis, and Fotis Ifantidis

2013 The Other Acropolises: Multi-temporality and the Persistence of the Past. In *The Oxford Handbook of the Archaeology of the Contemporary World*, edited by Paul Graves-Brown and Rodney Harrison, pp. 358–381. Oxford University Press, Oxford.

Harris, Robert

2006 *Imperium: A Novel of Ancient Rome.* Simon & Schuster, New York.

Harvard University Gazette

2002 Paleontologist, Author Gould Dies at 60. http://news.harvard.edu/gazette/2002/05.16/99-gould.html, accessed May 1, 2015.

Hodder, Ian

2012 *Entangled: An Archaeology of the Relationships between Humans and Things.* Wiley-Blackwell, London.

Holmberg, Kim, and Mike Thelwall

2014 Disciplinary Differences in Twitter Scholarly Communication. *Scientometrics* 101(2): 1027–1042.

Holtorf, Cornelius

2002 Notes on the Life History of a Pot Sherd. *Journal of Material Culture* 7(1): 49–72.

2005 *From Stonehenge to Las Vegas: Archaeology as Popular Culture.* Altamira Press, Lanham, Maryland.

Iannone, Gyles

2014 *The Great Maya Droughts in Cultural Context: Case Studies in Resilience and Vulnerability.* University Press of Colorado, Boulder.

Jameson, F.

2015 The Aesthetics of Singularity. *New Left Review* 92: 101–132.

Johnson, Marilyn

2014 *Lives in Ruins: Archaeologists and the Seductive Lure of Human Rubble.* Harper, New York.

Kopytoff, Igor

1986 The Cultural Biography of Things: Commoditization as Process. In *The Social Life of Things: Commodities in Cultural Perspective*, edited by Arjun Appadurai, pp. 64–91. Cambridge University Press, Cambridge.

Latour, Bruno

2005 *Reassembling the Social: An Introduction to Actor-Network-Theory.* Oxford University Press, Oxford

Layard, Austen Henry

1848 *Nineveh and its Remains.* Murray, London.

Letierce, Julie, Alexandre Passant, John Breslin, and Stefan Decker

2010 Understanding How Twitter is Used to Spread Scientific Messages. *Proceedings of the WebSci10: Extending the Frontiers of Society On-Line.* Raleigh, NC.

Lowenthal, David
   1985   *The Past is a Foreign Country*. Cambridge University Press, New York.
Lupton, Deborah
   2014   *"Feeling Better Connected": Academics' Use of Social Media*. News & Media Research
          Centre, University of Canberra.
Macaulay, David
   1979   *Motel of the Mysteries*. Houghton Mifflin, Boston.
Mann, Charles C.
   2005   *1491: New Revelations of the Americas before Columbus*. Knopf, New York
McGrath, Charles
   2010   How Cancer Acquired Its Own Biographer. *The New York Times*, 8 November 2010.
          (Retrieved 22 December 2012.)
Meltzer, David J.
   2009   *First Peoples in a New World: Colonizing Ice Age America*. University of California
          Press, Berkeley.
Michener, James
   1965   *The Source*. Random House, New York.
Milligan, Markus, and Jim Mower (eds.)
   2015   *Heritage Daily*. Online Magazine, http://www.heritagedaily.com, accessed April 15,
          2015.
Morris, Ian
   2010   *Why the West Rules – For Now: The Patterns of History and What They Reveal about
          the Future*. Profile Books, London.
Mukherjee, Siddhartha
   2010   *The Emperor of All Maladies*. Scribner, New York.
Nelson, Sarah Milledge
   1997   *Gender in Archaeology: Analyzing Power and Prestige*. AltaMira Press, Walnut Creek,
          California.
Olsen, Bjørnar, Michael Shanks, Timothy Webmoor, and Christopher Witmore
   2012   *Archaeology: The Discipline of Things*. University of California Press, Berkeley.
Praetzellis, Adrian
   2003   *Dug to Death: A Tale of Archaeological Method and Mayhem*. AltaMira Press, Walnut
          Creek.
   2011   *Death by Theory: A Tale of Mystery and Archaeological Theory*. Revised Edition.
          AltaMira Press, Lanham.
Pringle, Heather Anne
   2001   *The Mummy Congress: Science, Obsession, and the Everlasting Dead*. Hyperion, New
          York.
Pryor, Francis
   2003   *Britain B.C.: Life in Britain and Ireland before the Romans*. HarperCollins, London.
   2004   *Britain A.D.: A Quest for Arthur, England, and the Anglo-Saxons*. HarperCollins,
          London.
Rathje, William L., and Cullen Murphy
   1992   *Rubbish! The Archaeology of Garbage*. HarperCollins, New York.

Renfrew, Colin

    1973   *Before Civilization: The Radiocarbon Revolution and Prehistoric Europe.* Knopf, New York.

    1986   Varna and the Emergence of Wealth in Prehistoric Europe. In *The Social Life of Things: Commodities in Cultural Perspective*, edited by Arjun Appadurai, pp. 141–168. Cambridge University Press, Cambridge.

    1988   *Archaeology and Language: The Puzzle of Indo-European Origins.* Cambridge University Press, New York.

Rockman, Marcy, and Joe Flatman (eds.)

    2012   *Archaeology in Society: Its Relevance in the Modern World.* Springer, New York.

Rudwick, Martin J. S.

    1972   *The Meaning of Fossils: Episodes in the History of Paleontology.* Macdonald, London.

Ryzewski, Krysta, and John F. Cherry

    2012   Communities and Archaeology under the Soufrière Hills Volcano on Montserrat, West Indies. *Journal of Field Archaeology* 37(4): 316–327.

Salameh, Elias

    2004   Ancient Water Supply Systems and Their Relevance for Today's Society in Jordan. In *Men of Dikes and Canals: The Archaeology of Water in the Middle East*, edited by Hans-Dieter Bienert and Jutta Häser, pp. 285–290. Marie Leidorf, Rahden.

Smith, Joseph L.

    1956   *Tombs, Temples, and Ancient Art.* University of Oklahoma Press, Norman, OK.

Sobin, Gustaf

    1999   *Luminous Debris: Reflecting on Vestige in Provence and Languedoc.* University of California Press, Berkeley.

Spencer, Charles S.

    2000   Prehispanic Water Management and Agricultural Intensification in Mexico and Venezuela: Implications for Contemporary Ecological Planning. In *Imperfect Balance: Landscape Transformations in the Precolumbian Andes*, edited by David L. Lentz, pp. 147–178. Cambridge University Press, New York.

Stanford, Dennis J., and Bruce A. Bradley

    2012   *Across Atlantic Ice: The Origin of America's Clovis Culture.* University of California Press, Berkeley.

Strathern, Marilyn

    1988   *The Gender of the Gift: Problems with Women and Problems with Society in Melanesia.* University of California Press, Berkeley.

Toubert, Pierre

    1973   *Les structures du Latium médiéval: le Latium méridional et la Sabine du IXe siècle à la fin du XIIe siècle.* École française de Rome, Rome.

Trowel Blazers

    2015   *Trowel Blazers: Women in Archaeology, Geology, and Palaeontology.* Web Page: http:// trowelblazers.com, accessed April 15, 2015, curated by B. Hasset, V. Herridge, S. Pilaar Birch, and R. Wragg Sykes.

Verini, James

    2015   *Love and Ruin.* https://read.atavist.com/loveandruin, accessed April 19, 2015.

Von Däniken, Erich

    1968   *Chariots of the Gods? Unsolved Mysteries of the Past.* Bantam Books, New York.

Wengrow, David
    2010   *What Makes Civilization? The Ancient Near East and the Future of the West.* Oxford University Press, Oxford.

Wheeler, R. E. Mortimer
    1954   *Archaeology from the Earth.* Clarendon Press, Oxford.

Young, Peter A.
    2012   In Praise of the Storytellers. In *Archaeology in Society: Its Relevance in the Modern World*, edited by Marcy Rockman and Joe Flatman, pp. 59–62. Springer, New York.

Yourcenar, Marguerite
    1954   *Memoirs of Hadrian.* (First published as *Mémoires d'Hadrien*, Paris 1951.) Farrar, Straus and Young, New York.

Index